KV-656-379

Making The Most Of Appraisal

Career and Professional Development Planning for Lecturers

Graham Webb

KOGAN PAGE

MERTHYR TYDFIL COLLEGE

10058

371.144
ACC 11375

Teaching and Learning in Higher Education Series
Series Editor: John Stephenson

500 Tips for Tutors Phil Race and Sally Brown
Assessing Learners in Higher Education Sally Brown and Peter Knight
Case Studies on Teaching in Higher Education Peter Schwartz and Graham Webb
Making the Most of Appraisal Graham Webb
Practical Pointers for University Teachers Bill Cox
Using Learning Contracts in Higher Education John Stephenson and
   Mike Laycock
Using Records of Achievement in Higher Education Alison Assiter and Eileen Shaw

Dedicated to Terry Crooks with sincere thanks for your encouragement and wholehearted support.

First published in 1994

Apart from any fair dealing for the purposes of research or private study, or criticism or review, as permitted under the Copyright, Designs and Patents Act, 1988, this publication may only be reproduced, stored or transmitted, in any form or by any means, with the prior permission in writing of the publishers, or in the case of reprographic reproduction in accordance with the terms of licences issued by the Copyright Licensing Agency. Enquiries concerning reproduction outside those terms should be sent to the publishers at the undermentioned address:

Kogan Page Limited
120 Pentonville Road
London N1 9JN

© Graham Webb, 1994

British Library Cataloguing in Publication Data

A CIP record for this book is available from the British Library.
ISBN 0 7494 1256 9

Typeset by Saxon Graphics Ltd, Derby

Printed and bound in Great Britain by Biddles Ltd,
Guildford and King's Lynn

Contents

Foreword

Some things in life are not really amenable to deliberate planning. Until recently, it was widely believed that one of those things was the career of an academic. I well remember a former colleague confessing that his career had grown up 'behind his back and under his feet'. Many of us, when we survey our curriculum vitae, feel the same way: it's almost as if our professional lives have evolved, spontaneously and unbidden, in unpredictable ways.

All this is changing. Whether we like it or not, universities are becoming more corporate, and their senior staff more overtly managerial. Strategic plans proliferate, personnel departments have given way to offices of human resource management, and informal chats with the head of department have been supplemented – and in some cases replaced – by formal staff development planning interviews. Universities today talk about career planning and succession planning like most other large organizations, and the 'old' approaches to recruitment and promotion are making way for more tightly controlled, equity-orientated and carefully documented systems.

It is not difficult to resent some of these changes, especially those which are seen to diminish academic freedom, to undermine collegiality and to erode other cherished aspects of academic life. In particular, the increasingly common practice of institutionalizing performance reviews (and sometimes linking them to tenure, promotion or salary advancement) can be seen not only as intrusive but as wrong-headed because so many aspects of academic life are unpredictable and thus difficult to control. But while there are many things which it is beyond our ability to influence there are also many things we can do to ensure that our careers are not as random and serendipitous as perhaps they were in the past. It is also important for us as academics to understand and participate fully in processes directed towards professional review and our own professional development. In this direct, personal and highly readable book, Graham Webb tries to show how the individual academic can take control of vital aspects of his or her academic life.

While in no way diminishing the complexity or integrity of academic work, Graham (himself a successful and well-regarded academic and academic staff developer) argues that members of academic staff *can* further their own career and professional development aspirations by taking up the opportunities offered by self-appraisal, and where circumstances permit, by periodic appraisal interview. Instead of feeling oppressed, Graham argues, academics can benefit from systematically reflecting on their careers, from methodically collecting information about their performance, and from being in a position to ask for specific help from the institution in pursuing their career and professional goals. Wherever possible, appraisal can then be incorporated by academics into their own cycles of review, renewal and professional development.

Making the Most of Appraisal is informed by both a detailed knowledge of the literature and by a great deal of practical experience with academics in various disciplines and at different points in their careers. It is illustrated throughout with case study vignettes which succeed in making important points in a direct and memorable way. As academic work becomes more complex, more demanding and more public, this book is an invitation to view the process of appraisal (self-appraisal and the appraisal interview) as an opportunity rather than a threat. It is the kind of perspective we require if we are to keep a sense of order, balance and optimism in our higher education institutions.

Professor P C Candy
Director, Academic Staff Development Unit,
Queensland University of Technology.
President, Higher Education Research and
Development Society of Australasia.

Acknowledgements

I would like to acknowledge my gratitude and thanks to the following institutions and people:

The University of Otago, for granting the sabbatical leave during which this book was conceived and, for the most part, written;

The Faculty of Education at Nottingham Trent University, and in particular Mike O'Neil, for hosting me and providing support during my sabbatical;

My colleagues in the Higher Education Development Centre at Otago University, for taking on the extra work associated with my absence on leave;

My mother and father, for sharing their home and making our stay in England both possible and enjoyable;

Helen Carley of Kogan Page for consistently good advice as the book developed;

Peter Schwartz, for exemplary proof reading and Trevor Day for thoughtful, detailed and constructive comment;

Brenda Smith, Rod McKay, Sally Hunter, Nicola Peart, Terry Crooks, Val Clifford, Rob Rabel, Neil Fleming, Jenny Lee, John Jones and Adele Graham for comment and advice;

The extended family of HERDSA for providing support and friendship. My apologies to fellow staff development professionals for the many omissions and for the superficiality with which some of the issues are treated;

Susan, Alan and Lauren, for putting up with me.

To all of you, thanks.

Preface

I have been an academic for over 20 years. During that time I have picked up some hints and tips from those around me concerning what it is to be an academic, what I should be doing and how I might judge if I am doing these things well. I am thinking here about teaching, research, administration and the many other tasks I have taken on. For the most part, however, it is true to say that I knew remarkably little about 'being an academic' when I started and that my knowledge grew rather slowly. In fact it was only when I became an academic staff developer that I began to get a clearer picture. I realized then that a great deal has been written about what academics do; about such things as career life-cycles, professional development, the evaluation of teaching and of research. I wish I had known this earlier in my career.

It is my hope that you will learn some things from this book which will allow you to understand better your own career and your own experiences of 'being an academic'. I hope that it will help you to appreciate your career in terms of where you are now and where you see yourself going in the future. I hope too that you gain some comfort from the discovery that you are not the first person to face problems which perplex you, problems such as, 'How do I know if I am teaching well?', or 'Why is it that I never seem to have enough time for research?'

In this book you will be introduced to some of the literature on academic careers, on teaching, research and a lecturer's other responsibilities. Having covered some basic ground, you will then be given the opportunity to confront your own position, to evaluate where you stand presently, and to make plans and set objectives for the future. I have also given some indication of further reading which you might like to follow up if you are interested. However, this book is not intended to be comprehensive, and whenever I have been faced with a decision to make between being detailed and comprehensive or keeping the argument short, direct and personal, I have attempted to choose the latter. My hope is that this book will at least provide a useful starting point.

I wish that I had been able to go through this kind of material when I started out as a lecturer. It would have helped me to draw my activities into clearer focus and it would possibly have assisted me to see my work and my career in a more balanced way. I also wish that I had talked to many more people about the concerns I had and asked them to tell me about their own experiences. I wish I had taken more chances and attempted to reap more of the rewards which collegiality can offer. I was usually too afraid to take those chances. I was afraid of showing up my own ignorance and shortcomings – that I was a poor teacher or that I was not publishing enough. As a staff developer I now see people who are in exactly the same position. They feel isolated, are afraid to disclose their own uncertainties and are convinced that all except them have a clear view of their careers, a firm grasp on teaching or an unproblematic programme of research. That is exactly how I used to feel.

It is intended that as you work through this book you will gain important insights into your own career and some fundamentals of your own position with respect to professional development. Reflection, evaluation and development are the hallmarks of professionalism, and it is in the spirit of promoting professional self-knowledge and professional development that this book is written. It is also written to be of use in appraisal interviews. It is argued that by working systematically through the book, you will prepare yourself far more thoroughly for an appraisal interview than you have probably ever done in the past. The degree to which you feel able to share the insights you develop is then up to you. Gaining the insight in the first place is the important thing, whether or not you decide to share it with an appraiser.

A growing commitment by lecturers to their own continuing professional development is something which I think should be encouraged and something which I believe will increase markedly in the years ahead. I hope that as part of the generation of academics to make this growing commitment to professional development, you will find the book to be both useful and provocative. I would appreciate receiving anything you might like to write concerning how useful you found the book to be or pointing out its shortcomings.

Dr Graham Webb
Director, Higher Education Development Centre
University of Otago
PO Box 56
Dunedin
New Zealand

February 1994

Chapter One

Introduction

Appraisal schemes

Over the past few years, appraisal has become a fact of life for lecturers and academic staff in higher education. The value of appraisal schemes and the motives behind their introduction may be variously interpreted. Some would argue that an appraisal scheme offers a positive framework within which members of staff can systematically reflect upon their careers and their professional development. Others would say that such schemes are an intrusion upon academic freedom and professionalism: they represent a crude attempt to impose control and outdated 'line management' practices.

Many would argue that there has been a political agenda behind the introduction of appraisal schemes. Politicians and their functionaries have been sceptical of the claims made by academics concerning the quality of the educational experience which higher education claims to offer. Many of today's decision makers, and their children, have experienced higher education for themselves. They may have been less than impressed at having to sit (with several hundred others) through boring lecture presentations. They may have been frustrated with poorly organized tutorials, or with a lecturer who was seemingly impossible to contact, remote and free from any personal concern for them. Academics are also accused of abusing the high degree of professional autonomy and flexibility in working conditions which they have traditionally enjoyed. In this view, they need to be 'reined-in', made more accountable, their performance monitored and regulated, the 'non-performers' identified and made to either shape-up or ship-out.

For the most part, senior academic managers appear to have been equivocal in their reactions to such views. Many have acquiesced to what they have seen as an inevitable political reality. Appraisal schemes have

15

therefore been introduced, often with little consultation and with little or no research evidence being produced to justify their likely effectiveness. Similarly, little thought seems to have been given to the appropriateness or relevance of imported private and public sector schemes for the purposes and contexts of higher education. The race has been on to produce the seemingly inevitable wads of 'appraisal forms', with little time being taken to consider either the consequences or the alternatives.[1]

This all sounds very negative. On the other side, and as we will see later in this book, the majority of academics take their teaching, research and other responsibilities very seriously. They work hard, accept professional responsibility for their actions, and are very interested in doing what they do, better. This being the case, it is no wonder that many higher education institutions have learned that for appraisal to stand any chance of success, it must have a *developmental* focus. So there has been a change in emphasis, with the appraisal interview generally being seen less and less as a 'backward looking' device for evaluation, performance-related reward, control and censure. Instead, it has been interpreted as a mechanism for collegial discussion, 'forward looking' in its concern for professional development.

In fact, of course, appraisal interviews are a curious mish-mash of both evaluation and development. This is hardly surprising, as some degree of evaluation is necessary in planning for development and in assessing the impact of any changes made. This *should* be part of normal professional practice. Indeed, it is hard to imagine academic pursuits such as teaching or research without at the same time thinking of people engaged in processes which cause them to reflect, evaluate, plan, act, monitor, learn and change what they do, and how they do it. This kind of process is surely a central and integral part of our professionalism as academics.

The move towards institutional appraisal schemes has brought the importance of such processes to the fore, but in changed circumstances. Somewhat informal and *ad hoc* processes of self-evaluation and development have been superseded by the formal process of institutional appraisal, and the notion of 'appraiser' and 'appraisee'. The role of 'appraiser' has been particularly contentious. Appraisers who are also heads of departments (or similar) have to develop a somewhat schizophrenic personality. In one guise they are colleagues, trying to be empathic, supportive and positive with regard to individual frailty, while in another, they have the power to withhold resources and respond negatively to applications for promotion. This creates problems for each of us in knowing how far we should expose our frailties, our deepest concerns or most cherished ambitions. Given these circumstances, what should we do?

The stance taken in this book is that institutional appraisal *can* represent an opportunity for you to consider your own professional development. In working through this book you will be able to reflect upon your own stage of career development and how you see your career progressing. You will be able to consider where you presently stand with regard to your own teaching, research and other responsibilities, and where you see yourself going with respect to each of these in the future. You will also be given some guidance on the appraisal interview itself and ways in which you might attempt to ensure its success. All of this can be of positive value to you, irrespective of how far you choose to share your own insights with your appraiser.

It is to be hoped that you are in a situation where you have no qualms about sharing your own insights or self-appraisal with the tried and trusted colleague who is your appraiser. If this is not the case, however, you will have to decide just how far you are prepared to go in revealing your own insights, and how far you judge it expedient to keep them to yourself. At worst (and this is one of the problems with appraisal to an institutionalized formula) you may choose to divulge little of value in the appraisal process, in the expectation of receiving little by way of sympathetic understanding from your appraiser in return. Appraisal under such circumstances becomes a meaningless paper-shuffling exercise, or a new site for the continuation of longstanding antagonisms and failures to communicate. Should this be the case, you may *still* derive much of value from working your way through this book, and perhaps sharing some of the insights or directions for development you see as valuable, with a colleague whom you *do* respect and trust: a surrogate appraiser or collegial adviser, as it were.

So, if your institutional appraisal scheme encourages you to take an honest look at your career to this point, and to plan for development in the future, then this is how appraisal for development is supposed to work. Using this book will help you in your preparation and planning for appraisal. However, if your judgement is that you cannot trust your institutional appraisal process, then there is still much to be gained by working through the activities in this book. Whatever blend you create between your institutional appraisal scheme and the insights you develop as you work through this book, the idea is that you will be 'making the most' of the opportunities which appraisal, of one kind or another, can offer.

Why bother when I have to be appraised anyway?

An obvious question for you to ask at this point is: 'Why should I bother to go through *more* appraisal when I have to be appraised each year anyway and this *already* takes up too much time?' There are various answers to this. First, and as suggested above, you have much to gain from reflection upon your career and developmental objectives as you work through this book, with none of the attendant risks or threats which might be associated with self-disclosure within the institutional scheme you are obliged to follow.

Second, institutional schemes are often weak when it comes to considering long- or medium-term objectives. They require you to commit yourself to short-term (next year's) and often spuriously quantified objectives, with little regard to how these fit your own longer-term objectives and aspirations. In fact some institutional schemes are very poor indeed, mistakenly confusing the concrete activity of filling in pre-determined boxes with the often difficult and messy process of self-appraisal and development.

Third, the institutional process is often rushed in the extreme; there is little time for serious reflection or for finding out about areas or directions in which you might wish to develop. The forms have to be in, the boxes ticked, the lines completed, signed and countersigned, with little regard for the thought or groundwork which *should* go into their completion.

Fourth, it is an unfortunate fact that many appraisers are themselves rather undeveloped when it comes to knowledge and understanding of, for example, studies regarding academic careers, and the evaluation of teaching and research. At best an appraiser might be able to offer you good and informed advice, or direct you towards other colleagues or an educational development unit for assistance in areas where he or she has little knowledge or experience. At worst, an appraiser might simply offer advice based upon his or her own prejudices, themselves born of ignorance. Taking the word of senior colleagues with regard to what constitutes successful teaching, for example, when they have taught in exactly the same way for 20 years, have never evaluated their own teaching, and are unfamiliar with the literature on the subject, may be problematic to say the least.

This book gives you the chance to reflect according to your own time schedule and to make considered judgements as to how you see your career progressing, and what you consider your developmental priorities to be. It is essentially a first step in terms of your own development and change, irrespective of the degree to which your use of it overlaps with the official scheme operated by the institution in which you work. However, there is little doubt that by working through this book, you will be in a much better position to address your own institutional appraisal interview when the time comes around.

How is the book organized?

The course taken in this book is first to ask you to consider where you are now and then where you think you are going, in terms of your career generally, your teaching, research and other responsibilities. Having established where you stand presently, you will be asked to consider your long-term and medium-term aspirations, and from these to set some shorter-term priorities. Each chapter presents information which it is hoped you will find both interesting and worthwhile in terms of setting the scene for you to consider your own position. Some questions will then be posed in order to provide you with the opportunity of stating your position and making you own plans. The best way to tackle these questions is to write down your responses, as this will help you to clarify your own thinking and to make explicit your ideas, which may presently be only hazy or tentative. If you want to start a file or notebook (on paper or disk), or to allocate a section of your diary for the task, then so much the better. At the end of the book we move on to the appraisal interview itself, and things you can do to help ensure that it works to your advantage; that you are clear about what it is you want to get out of the discussion, and about the consequences and further actions which should ensue.

One of the features of the book is the use of case studies of academics facing problems which tend to recur throughout higher education. The case studies and the people described are fictitious, or perhaps 'factitious' may be more accurate, in that they are based upon both my own personal experience, and experience gained while working with colleagues in my role as a staff developer. It is intended that the case studies will personalize the process, assist in the identification and clarification of problems and priorities, and help and encourage you in the consideration of your own position.

Finally, it should be said that the way in which the book is written suggests that you are undergoing an appraisal process for the first time. This might be the case. However, it is perhaps more likely that you will have undergone an institutional appraisal process already. If you *have* already completed an appraisal process with which you are fairly happy, you may find that you are in a good position to comment upon your plans and actions from *last* year: what actually happened and why. Wherever possible, you should endeavour to bring what you learned last year or previously into your plans for the future. If you are new to academia, new to teaching, new to research, new to administration, new to some other area of academic responsibility, or new to appraisal: welcome. If you have experience in each of these: welcome, and I wish you every success in integrating what you have learned so far with your plans for the future.

Note

1. If you are interested in reading more on criticisms of appraisal and 'managerialism', their inappropriateness for higher education, and alternative approaches to evaluation and accountability, see: Gitlin and Smyth, 1989; Moses, 1989; Smyth, 1989.

Chapter Two

Where am I now with my career?

Introduction

In this chapter you will be encouraged to consider where you stand presently with regard to your career generally. Each one of us can legitimately claim to be a special case in terms of our careers. There are a number of routes into lecturing as a career, many aspects to what we do as lecturers, many changes of circumstance, possibilities and challenges which confront us during the course of our careers. There are also dissimilarities in the cultures which we encounter within differing educational and research institutions, and among the disciplines and practices which comprise modern educational institutions.

This having been said, it is also possible to discern regularities. In terms of career development it is often possible to distinguish an early stage of establishing ourselves in the career and of obtaining tenure or confirmation of appointment. Even though tenure has become less of an issue in many institutions, the need for lecturers to establish themselves in the early stages of their careers has remained as a difficult but very important stage which continues to confront us.

Following this, the pursuit of promotion remains a recurring theme up to or beyond attainment of the career grade (the point which most staff are expected to reach but not advance beyond). Mid-career re-evaluation is also a common experience, particularly with regard to the importance of research. Similarly, the anticipation of retirement can cause us to reflect on what we want to achieve in the time remaining before retirement, and whether or not we see ourselves fulfilling a continuing academic role after retirement.

It is important for you to have an overall context from which to view where you presently stand with regard to your career, but unfortunately, institutional appraisal schemes do not always encourage this. There is always the pressure of time, of substantive points to decide concerning the courses you will teach next year, what you expect to publish, etc., so that the overall context for your activities can easily be lost. Having a clear appreciation of where you stand in terms of your career will help you better prioritize and plan the activities you wish to undertake. It is also more likely that if you have this clear understanding yourself, you will be better able to explain the thinking behind your plans to your appraiser.

General career issues are the focus of this chapter. To help in considering these, we will look at a number of case studies of people at differing points in their careers. You will be able to assess 'where they are' and what issues and problems confront them. While the cases are fictitious, they have been informed by actual events and experiences. The idea is that it is often easier to view objectively, analyse and offer advice on other people's careers than it is on one's own career. By considering the case studies you may be better placed to interpret your own career in a slightly wider context than might otherwise have been likely. You will be invited to comment on the situations and the issues which are raised, and which many lecturers face, as a precursor to identifying your own career position: of describing exactly where you presently see yourself and your own career.

Following on from this you will then be encouraged to examine how you see your career developing in the future, what your goals are and what you are trying to achieve in your career. Looking forward and planning what you want to achieve in your career is the major concern of the next chapter: 'Where am I going with my career?' Before moving on to the case studies we need to be clear about some of the terms which will be used.

Career position, career and professional development

Career position

While career or academic rank refers to categories such as professor or lecturer, I will use *career position* to denote a particular place on the career 'ladder'. Third increment on the lecturer scale or top of the senior lecturer scale are examples of career position.[1]

Career development

The term *career development* can have either a narrow or a wider connotation. In the narrow meaning, it is often used to mean progress up a particular career ladder from one career position to another. This narrow meaning is the one used in this chapter. It is based on the notion that the reader has chosen a career as a lecturer in higher education, and will stay *within* the career structure which this implies. Of course lecturers *do* move in and out of this career structure. They move in and out of industry, commerce, public and private sector research agencies. They also take up fellowships of various kinds, as well as unpaid leave for professional or other purposes. Herein lies the wider meaning, which views the career development of a person as a whole, whether within or outside the career structures of higher education. Again, for the purposes of this book, we will be concerned with career development *within* higher education.

Professional development

Both career position and career development may be distinguished from *professional development*. In using the term professional development, I will be referring to the process by which we monitor and try to improve upon the various things we do in our work, such as lecturing to large classes, taking small group tutorials, publishing papers or administrating a course.

In theory, and counter to commonroom gossip, the three *can* and indeed *should* be related. The three things are not synonymous, however, and there is often no blindingly clear relationship between them. For example, the steps we take in professional development may help to improve our current career position, and thus the development of our careers. On the other hand, many at the career grade who recognize that they have little prospect of further promotion are actively involved in their own continuing professional development.

Career case studies

Why bother to look at career case studies? There are two reasons. First, as previously mentioned, they are a good way of encouraging you to take an objective view of your own career position and possibilities for career development. They widen your appreciation of the context within which you interpret your own situation.

Second, considering case studies may help you in the formal appraisal process, by giving you an insight into how your appraiser might be looking at you. A common training activity for appraisers is role playing with specially written cases displaying features which commonly occur at particular career positions. These cases can be thought of as career positions stereotypes.

It is profoundly human to want to categorize and stereotype people, but it is also dangerous, especially when the major criterion is something as dubious as career position. Nevertheless, appraisers will certainly have their own prejudices with respect to an individual's career position. For example, they will have their own thoughts on how one should go about securing tenure, making progress though the lecturer or senior lecturer scale, what counts for substantive promotion, what someone at the career grade level should be doing, etc. They will apply their own concepts of what makes for successful career development. It is to be hoped that those prejudices will be refined and changed during the appraisal process, but the initial positions taken can have a powerful influence. It is to your advantage to be familiar with the kind of stereotypical case studies upon which your appraiser is likely to have been trained.

What then are some typical career positions, and their consequences for career and professional development? We will consider five such cases. The cases are stereotyped, but you may be able to discern something of the particular nature of the person within the case. You may be able to identify some aspects which fit with colleagues you know. You may also see some features of your own position either now, in the past, or in the possible future.

Try to imagine or to visualize the people in the cases, and to identify with them as they prepare for an appraisal interview. Each person in the case has been assigned male or female gender, the first, for example, being Barbara Langton. More stereotypes tend to come into play as soon as gender is introduced. The cases could have been written in the alternative gender, for example Brian Langton in the first case. If you find that you can more easily identify with the person as Brian, rather than Barbara, and similarly with the other cases, then please read the case accordingly.

Essentially the same questions are posed at the end of each case. The questions have been repeated to encourage you to respond to each case as you read it. It is a good idea, therefore, to pencil in your responses immediately after having read the case, rather than waiting until you have read all of the cases. A short discussion of the cases follows this activity.

BARBARA (BRIAN) LANGTON

Barbara Langton is a relative newcomer to lecturing in higher education. She has been at the university for two years, having been appointed low on the lecturer scale. She will soon be considered for tenure. Because an unusually large number of staff from the department have been away for various reasons over the last couple of years, Barbara has had a very heavy teaching load. Barbara took this on willingly, and has spent many hours on improving the organization and teaching of the courses which she has taken over. She was not very impressed by the quality of the organization and structure of the courses she inherited. On top of that, she has also developed a new course in her own area.

Barbara has developed a reputation within the department as being a good teacher, and this has been borne out in the student evaluations of teaching she has taken of her courses. She says that her primary responsibility is to organize and teach the department's courses well and so that is why she has directed her efforts here. Barbara considers that she is now getting on top of developing the courses she is teaching and that in another one or two years she will have things under control.

Barbara has not published anything of significance since joining the department. She intended to write up the outcomes from her postgraduate work but has not done so. She is working in an area where it is common to seek funding for research projects, but she has not had the time to apply for a research grant. Barbara has not viewed any of this as being a problem as there will be time to turn towards research when she has sorted out the teaching side of her work. She is now beginning to wonder if this is really the case.

Barbara has been quite happy to shoulder the burden of other staff being away and has enjoyed the part she has played in developing and improving courses in the department. She knows that her own research has suffered because of this, but up until now has believed that there will be plenty of time to catch up when the job of improving the organization and teaching of courses is complete. As far as she is concerned, she has been doing the job which was most pressing and which the department most needed. Barbara still has a very heavy teaching load, but having put in all this work already, she is very reluctant to pass over courses to others, especially as it would be to the very people who had not made a good job of them in the first place. Barbara is now beginning to be a little concerned that the efforts she has put into teaching may not compensate for her neglect of research.

- *Imagine you are Barbara and that you are in the appraisal interview. The appraiser asks you to describe where you presently stand with regard to your career. How would you respond?*
- *If you were Barbara, what would you do to improve your position? What outcomes would you be looking for as a result of the appraisal interview?*
- *What do you think will be the appraiser's agenda in the appraisal interview with Barbara?*
- *Does Barbara's case raise any areas of similarity or resonance with your own position? How, in what ways?*

MICHAEL (MICHELLE) RICHARDS

This is the second year that Michael Richards has been at the institution and he will be coming up for tenure soon. He was appointed some way up the lecturer scale, having had previous commercial and industrial experience. Michael is now 35 years old and is enjoying the flexibility of an academic position and the opportunities this affords for time with his family, to which he is very committed. He does not mix much with other people in the department and has not made any friendships with his colleagues. Michael is well on the way to completing a PhD; he published a couple of papers last year and has considerable PhD research material to use for future publication. He has also recently been asked by the head of department to take over the coordination and administration of a course which he and a number of other people teach.

Michael always prepares his lectures thoroughly and meticulously, using lots of overhead projector transparencies and handouts. He has never considered himself to be a 'great' teacher, but neither has he had any indication that he is any better or any worse than others in the department. At least that was the case until the end of last year, when the colleagues with whom he shares a large first-year lecture course suggested that they should all ask for a student evaluation of teaching. The results from this are confidential to each staff member, although some of the lecturers have talked about their evaluations openly, while others, including Michael, have not done so. In fact, when the results came back, Michael received a poor rating, and he has been too embarrassed to discuss this with his colleagues (not really knowing them personally) or with his head of department. Michael realizes that the question of tenure will soon be coming up but is not clear what place teaching evaluations will have in this.

- *Imagine you are Michael and that you are in the appraisal interview. The appraiser asks you to describe where you presently stand with regard to your career. How would you respond?*
- *If you were Michael, what would you do to improve your position? What outcomes would you be looking for as a result of the appraisal interview?*
- *What do you think will be the appraiser's agenda in the appraisal interview with Michael?*
- *Does Michael's case raise any areas of similarity or resonance with your own position? How, in what ways?*

JANET (JOHN) SMITH

Janet Smith was appointed at the bottom of the lecturer scale some years ago, and she has advanced step by step. She has been awarded tenure. Janet has published a sizeable, single-authored book and about 12 papers in good journals. She has regularly taken student evaluations of her teaching, and the results of these concerning her lectures have been very impressive. This is noteworthy since these courses are not strictly in her own area of specialism. The evaluations she has had of her tutorials (small group discussions) have been satisfactory, but less impressive. Janet is involved in a small number of departmental committees where she is seen as being very efficient, but also somewhat confrontational and brusque at times. She admits that she does 'not suffer fools gladly'.

Janet is ambitious to advance and is frustrated that she is not advancing quickly enough. She sees people elsewhere within the university being promoted to or appointed at higher levels than her own, without equivalent qualifications, publications or excellence in teaching. Janet feels that she is doing everything 'right' but despite this she faces years of crawling up the lecturer scale, step by step. She feels frustrated and disillusioned by this. Janet wonders if the head of department really appreciates how good her teaching evaluations are or how positively her book and papers have been received.

It does not seem to matter what Janet does, she is trapped on the scale. She is beginning to think that she will have to leave to get promotion and has been taking a keener interest in job advertisements. She does not really want to leave as she enjoys the courses she is teaching and would like to develop a new course in her own specialism. However, it is hard to be enthusiastic about this when she feels so frustrated with her career.

- *Imagine you are Janet and that you are in the appraisal interview. The appraiser asks you to describe where you presently stand with regard to your career. How would you respond?*
- *If you were Janet, what would you do to improve your position? What outcomes would you be looking for as a result of the appraisal interview?*

- *What do you think will be the appraiser's agenda in the appraisal interview with Janet?*
- *Does Janet's case raise any areas of similarity or resonance with your own position? How, in what ways?*

PAUL (PAULINE) WHITING

Paul Whiting has been a lecturer for many years. He has been at the career grade for a considerable time but has never applied for promotion beyond it. Paul has not published anything at all in the last four years and is not engaged in any research at the moment. He has plenty of good ideas for research and unselfishly gives his time and ideas to both colleagues and students. Paul is very affable and well liked within the department. He is now 50 years old, with a grown-up family and no thoughts of leaving the institution.

Paul professes an interest in and commitment to teaching and has been heard to say: 'My life is teaching and students'. He approaches his teaching with great enthusiasm, and tries to pass on this enthusiasm to his students. He has never taken a student evaluation of his teaching as this was unheard of in his day. He regards himself as a good teacher, however, despite having heard the odd remark from students concerning his 'going too fast' and 'getting a bit carried away'. Paul has recently become enthusiastic about computers and the possibility of computer-assisted learning for students. However, he has had enthusiasms in the past which have come to nothing. Paul undertakes some administrative tasks within the department, but no more than other people at his level who are publishing regularly.

Paul is actually quite equivocal about his work, his position in the department, and goals for the rest of his professional life. While appearing blasé about the appraisal interview, Paul is becoming somewhat concerned about moves towards 'account-ability' within the university. With some encouragement, therefore, he would be quite pleased to get moving again in one way or another. He has thought about doing something on 'teaching', perhaps the idea of using computers in his course. On the other hand, he can argue that although he may not be the most dynamic person in the university, he is doing a reasonable job, and there are certainly others he knows who are doing less.

Paul could also be more involved in administration. He has many personal characteristics which make him popular within the department. This may be the reason why the head of department has raised the possibility with him of taking on some of the appraisal interviews within the department next year. It is a fairly large department, and the head is keen to shed some of the load. Paul has not responded to this yet, and the suggestion was pretty vague.

- *Imagine you are Paul and that you are in the appraisal interview. The appraiser asks you to describe where you presently stand with regard to your career. How would you respond?*
- *If you were Paul, what would you do to improve your position? What outcomes would you be looking for as a result of the appraisal interview?*
- *What do you think will be the appraiser's agenda in the appraisal interview with Paul?*

- *Does Paul's case raise any areas of similarity or resonance with your own position? How, in what ways?*

CHARLES (CAROL) ROSS

Charles Ross has had a distinguished academic career. He was appointed to the university at senior lecturer level nearly 30 years ago and has continued to build a record of satisfactory teaching and strong research productivity. He was promoted rapidly, eventually being awarded a personal chair, and some 18 years ago (at the age of 44) was awarded the second established chair in his department.

Since that time, Charles has become increasingly heavily involved in departmental administration and has also gained a reputation for effectiveness in committee work at faculty and university level. He continued to publish steadily until about ten years ago, but since then has published very little. He continues to teach at all levels, with a slightly reduced load because of his responsibilities as head of department.

Charles Ross has enjoyed his time as a professor. It has been a stimulating challenge to guide and build the department, and he has also received considerable kudos for committee and administrative work beyond the department. The latter included three years as dean of the faculty about 15 years ago. Charles has also taken up leadership roles at national level in his discipline, and ten years ago he had two years on the board of the international association of scholars in his speciality. However, he has noticed that such involvement beyond the university has declined in the last few years. He attributes this to a lack of research involvement and productivity.

Charles has made a number of attempts to resume an active research programme, but it seems that other urgent tasks always seem to come along to destroy any sense of progress, before he ever really gets going. He has come to the conclusion that it will be necessary to drop most of his administrative commitments if he is to gain sufficient momentum to regenerate his research. This poses a problem, because he enjoys leadership, and is not confident that there is currently an alternative leader of sufficient stature within the department. A particular reader/associate professor in the department is making good progress, and could be ready for the headship in a few years' time.

While Charles has enjoyed most of what he has been doing in the past few years, he is feeling increasingly upset that he has not been able to maintain a productive research programme. This is because he wants to continue to have an academic life after retirement. In order for this to happen, however, he does not think that he can afford to carry on as he is at present.

- *Imagine you are Charles and that you are in the appraisal interview. The appraiser asks you to describe where you presently stand with regard to your career. How would you respond?*
- *If you were Charles, what would you do to improve your position? What outcomes would you be looking for as a result of the appraisal interview?*
- *What do you think will be the appraiser's agenda in the appraisal interview with Charles?*
- *Does Charles' case raise any areas of similarity or resonance with your own position? How, in what ways?*

Comments on the case studies

Here then are some examples of people at various career positions, preparing for the appraisal process while facing both career development and professional development issues. In these cases, we can clearly see how career and professional development are enmeshed. We have some stereotypical examples of problems which lecturers encounter at various stages of their careers.[2]

Barbara and Michael have both been appointed relatively recently and are facing the challenge of establishing themselves in their positions and securing tenure. They are at a fairly similar stage. However, they have dissimilar professional development problems. Barbara is weak in terms of the research she has published since her appointment, even though she has good grounds for arguing that the teaching duties she has performed have been of major benefit to the department. She really needs to know how serious a threat not having published is to her case for tenure. Michael, on the other hand, has encountered a problem in student evaluations of his part of a large first-year lecture course, and he needs to know whether his teaching will be raised as an issue in his bid for tenure.

Problems such as these are common with younger or new staff, who often find themselves in the unenviable position of having a heavy teaching load together with considerable pressure to publish quickly. At the same time they may be coping with a young family (new baby), settling into a new work environment, possibly a new location, finding accommodation and attempting to construct a new social life, all on a depressingly small salary. In such a situation, the need to be focused on the necessities for self-preservation is paramount.

Both Barbara and Michael need to recognize that their current problems can clearly be interpreted within the context of their stage of career development. Once they have established themselves and gained tenure, they will be able to adopt a more measured and balanced approach to their professional development. Each could benefit from professional development advice, one concerning getting started on research and publishing, the other on large group teaching.

Neither Janet nor Paul face such an immediately threatening situation, and their problems are somewhat different from those of Barbara and Michael. Janet is concerned for promotion, which she sees as being overdue because of her strong performance in both research and teaching. She needs to know how she stands with regard to promotion from her current career position, and to weigh up the pros and cons of looking for an alternative position elsewhere. With regard to professional development, she may also be interested in learning something about small group teaching, why it is that the student evaluations she receives in this area are not as good as those she receives for lecturing, and what she can do about it.

Paul is beginning to realize that he should make some changes in his professional life, even though these may have little impact on his chances of promotion. Although he is committed to teaching he has not attempted to evaluate his teaching, and thus to find where his strengths and weaknesses lie. In terms of research, he has not been productive for some time, and he is probably beginning to realize the consequences of this for his standing within the department, and for his own self-regard. He may consider getting back into research in his specialist area or, for example, merging his interest in teaching and the use of computer-assisted learning by developing a project in this area.

Finally, Charles Ross is looking ahead to retirement and to continuing to play an active role in some capacity or other after he retires. He presently sees the only way of accomplishing this to be in terms of establishing an active research programme once more. This will obviously not be easy, especially at the international level where he was once prominent, and as he does not see any possibility of relinquishing leadership of the department in the near future. He may thus be looking to re-examine the time scale for handing over leadership of the department, to re-establishing his links with the international bodies on which he once served, and perhaps seeking a period of leave during which he could redirect his career.

Your career

It is to be hoped that by considering these cases you will have begun to interpret your own career position a little more clearly, and in a slightly wider context. As I said earlier, it is always easier to analyse and offer advice on other people's careers, and harder to take an objective view of one's own. But that is precisely what we have been working towards in this chapter, and it is now time for you to consider a number of questions regarding your own career.

I would suggest that you take a little time over each one and write down a response. The main benefit to be obtained from this kind of exercise is in making explicit (ie, writing down) thoughts which may be somewhat hazy. The act of writing them down can help enormously in clarifying and organizing your thoughts.

- *Did any of the case studies present areas of similarity with your own career position? What were these areas? In considering the case studies did any other areas concerning your own career position occur to you?*
- *Imagine that you are in the appraisal interview and the appraiser asks you to describe where you presently stand with regard to your career. How would you respond – how would you describe your career position?*
- *Where do you consider you stand **at this moment** with regard to promotion or tenure? Upon what do you base your opinion, and how adequate do you consider this or these sources to be?*
- *What could you do to improve your present position? What outcomes will you be looking for as a result of your appraisal interview?*
- *What do you think will be the appraiser's agenda in your appraisal interview?*
- *Is there anyone you can talk to informally regarding your own interpretation of your career position? Would it be worthwhile to discuss this with a colleague or colleagues whose opinions you trust and respect?*

Notes

1. Rough equivalents of career rank for different countries and institutions:

UK Universities	UK Universities (former Polytechnics)	Australasian Universities	North American Universities
Professor	Professor	Professor	Professor
Reader/ Senior Lecturer	Reader/ Principal Lecturer	Associate Professor	Professor
Lecturer B	Senior Lecturer	Senior Lecturer	Associate Professor
Lecturer A	Lecturer II	Lecturer	Assistant Professor
	Lecturer I	Assistant/ Associate Lecturer	Instructor

2. There are a number of metaphors in use with regard to what an academic may typically experience during his or her career. 'The seasons of the year' or 'four seasons' metaphor is one example, in which spring, summer, autumn and winter can be used to interpret the academic's position and inclination at a given time. Writing from an American higher education perspective, Lee Knefelkamp (1990) talks of the 'seasons of academic life'. 'Life cycle' is another, and there has been quite a lot of academic research on the 'life cycle of the teacher'. Sikes *et al* (1985, Ch 2), for example, construct five typical phases for a teacher, based upon age. Within higher education, and particularly with regard to research, Becher (1989) identifies three typical stages as 'the achievement of independence', 'the mid-life crisis' and the 'end-point of active research'. These will be considered in more detail later in this book. We should bear in mind, however, that what is regarded as 'typical' is usually typical for men rather than women, as pointed out by writers such as Heather-Jane Robertson (1992).

Chapter Three

Where am I going with my career?

Introduction

In this chapter we move on from 'where you are now' to consider where you may be going with your career. This might seem a pointless exercise, to which the only sensible response is, 'How could I possibly know?' The route by which you entered lecturing, or the changes which have happened to you since you first started, may certainly appear to have been due more to chance than to any explicit planning on your part. People change specialisms, subject areas, institutions and geographical locations according to opportunities or events which are, to some extent, beyond their control. There is no reason to suppose that by making your career objectives explicit at this point, you will either ensure that these objectives are realized, or that you will keep these same objectives in the future.

Recognizing all of this does not prevent you from seeking to understand what your ambitions and aspirations are at this moment. The real lesson to be learned from serendipity is that career self-appraisal needs to be undertaken *frequently*, rather than never. When events in the past conspired to offer you opportunities, it was almost certainly your conscious plans, efforts and achievements which put you in a position to be able to take advantage of them. Similarly, it is the plans and efforts you make *now* which will enable you to take advantage of events in the future.

As you prepare for your appraisal interview it is important that you have a good idea of where you are going in the medium to long term. As I have said previously, it is very easy in an appraisal interview to be drawn straight into a discussion of the activities you see yourself pursuing next year. These activities *can* be a simple continuation of what you have been doing in the past. In fact the less adequately you prepare for an appraisal interview, the more this is likely to be the case. But appraisal offers you the opportunity to take a longer-term view than this. It offers the opportunity for you to step back from the immediacy of what you are doing now, and allows you to consider a wider range of possibilities than might normally occur in your day-to-day routine. To be well prepared to discuss 'where you see yourself going' in an appraisal interview is to have thought out beforehand how your plans for next year make sense in terms of your longer-term career objectives.

Two notes of caution: structures and optimism

Making plans for the future is an exhilarating exercise. There is nothing wrong with that, and indeed it is hard to imagine how we could live without an optimism that our futures will be happy and worthwhile. However, it is worth entering two notes of caution before embarking on the enterprise of planning for the future.

First, our actions take place within structures. Although the structures change with circumstances, and as people question and challenge them, we are better able to form our plans for the future if we appreciate the nature of structures within which we are located. For example, Donald Bligh (1990) notes how staffing policies in British universities dating from the 1960s have led to present career rank distributions with regard to age. It is worth reproducing, in Table 3.1, part of the table which Bligh constructs to show age distributions by academic rank, and quoting his interpretation at some length.

Table 3.1 *Percentage full-time non-clinical academic staff in British universities in 1989 analysed by age group and rank*

Age	Professors	Readers and Senior Lecturers	Lecturers	Others	Total
Under 25	–	–	48	52	1
25–29	0	0	86	14	5
30–34	0	2	95	3	9
35–39	3	13	83	1	14
40–44	8	26	65	0	20
45–49	13	35	51	0	20
50–54	19	41	40	0	16
55–59	27	39	34	0	9
over 59	39	32	29	0	5
Total	13	26	59	2	100

Source: Bligh, 1990, p. 180 (Universities Statistical Record). Percentages rounded to the nearest whole number.

The bunching of staff in their forties . . . reflects stringent staffing policies since the cuts in 1981. Early retirement schemes were introduced for the over-fifties. Furthermore, since that date nearly 20 per cent of academic staff under the age of 30 leave in any given year while the corresponding figure before 1981 was only 1 per cent. The university lecturer scale is a long one with annual increments in salary for seventeen years. Consequently universities cannot afford to appoint young staff on permanent contracts and most of the best brains drain away after contracts of three to five years . . . . Most lecturers must wait until their forties before they are promoted. Many don't get it even then and a good proportion in their fifties have taken advantage of early retirement schemes . . . . There is a similar age bunching in the public sector but it is less acute . . . (Bligh, 1990, pp. 180–81.)

Bligh notes how these age-rank profiles are also found in the British universities which were formerly polytechnics, and it may be added that somewhat similar profiles also pertain in Australasia and North America.

Another structural factor relates to the position of women in higher education. Bligh quotes the percentage distribution of women in British universities by academic rank for 1989 as follows: professors 3 per cent; readers and senior lecturers 8 per cent; lecturers 21 per cent; others 41 per cent; total 19 per cent (compared with 12 per cent in 1978).

Using results from his 1976 and 1989 surveys of the staffs of British universities and polytechnics, Halsey (1992) has commented at some length on a number of structural factors in academic careers. Here are some extracts.

On gender:

. . . women spent a greater proportion of their time than men teaching undergraduates (*35.2 per cent versus 33.1 per cent*) . . . and correspondingly they spent rather less of their working time in research activity (*20.8 per cent versus 23.2 per cent*) . . . men do more supervising of research students than do women (*70 per cent versus 56 per cent*). (p. 227, italicized figures added from elsewhere in the report).

On class origin:

. . . the odds on coming from a middle-class family are between one and a quarter and one and a half times greater among the professoriate than among the other academic ranks. (p. 203).

On Oxbridge:

. . . professors were three-quarters more likely . . . to have their doctorates from Oxford or Cambridge than were the other academic ranks (p. 205). . . . Oxford and Cambridge have played an important but not an especially meritocratic role in the recruitment of academics . . . (p. 206).

On teaching versus research:

Professors are more than twice as likely . . . as the non-professorial academics to give priority to research . . . . A person who has published over twenty articles is eight times more likely . . . to be found among the professors than a person who has published less than ten articles . . . three books more than doubles the odds (*of being a professor*) (p. 207, italicized text added).

On this last point, a general statement made by Over (1993) following his analysis of career advancement in Australian universities, has much validity for other countries too: 'career advancement was associated primarily with measures of research achievement' (p. 326).

Here then are some examples of structural factors and inequalities within which you will develop your career. You should be aware of them, and from your own experience you may well be able to add others. But structures result from our individual and collective efforts. They will be forced to change as we, the present generation of academics, challenge the inequalities we experience. This is true for women, but it is also true with regard to such things as the devaluing of teaching as opposed to research with respect to promotion. Women and men within higher education will constantly confront and dispute such inequalities as they plan and develop their careers for the future. (For further comment and readings regarding women's experience of academia, see Chapter 7 of this book.)

The second note of caution refers to a perennial problem in setting objectives and planning for the future. Such activity tends to encourage us to think of ourselves as 'clean pages' upon which we can be written anew. Like new diets, exercise programmes or books on 'how to get motivated', the new start can be extraordinarily liberating at first, only to flounder later as old histories catch up with the new 'us'.

Some philosophers talk of the past, the present and the future as moments, and that it is necessary to consider each in seeking an interpretation of any one. The second caution is, therefore, that in planning for the future it is better to do so with a realistic appreciation of ourselves, our strengths, weaknesses and achievements thus far, rather than thinking in terms of starting again from scratch. We are not the helpless victims of our own histories and of the structures within which we work, but nor can we completely disregard them in planning for the future. The relationship between what is there already and our own actions directed towards change, is a subtle one of ebb and flow, contest and negotiation.

With these words of caution in mind, let us return to the case studies which we encountered in the previous chapter, before we move on to your own career plans for the future.

Career plans for the case study examples

At this point you may wish to re-read the cases in the previous section. A brief summary of each case is also given below, before the people in the cases discuss how they see their careers developing, and the objectives which they intend to set for themselves. What then could the career plans of the people we encountered earlier look like? They might look something like this.

BARBARA (BRIAN) LANGTON

Summary reminder. *Barbara Langton is a relative newcomer to lecturing and will soon be facing a decision on tenure. She has had a very heavy teaching load, reorganizing and developing a number of courses. She has not published anything significant since joining the department, nor has she had the time to seek research funding.*

I don't know how far up the career ladder I will get. I have only been lecturing for a couple of years and so these are early days yet. At the moment I am not particularly ambitious to get to the top – prof/reader/assoc. prof/principal lecturer or whatever, but I would be disappointed not to reach the career grade. I like the job, particularly the teaching, and I am happy, for the time being anyway, to stay here as a lecturer, moving up the lecturer scale.

As to the shorter term, it is becoming increasingly clear to me how important it is that I put myself in a good position to have my appointment confirmed. Everything in the future really depends on this. I have been so busy settling in and getting all of my teaching in shape that I have not really thought about it very much before. I should really have been given more advice earlier, but things were left rather vague. I am only now beginning to realize how neglecting research, even though it was for the best of reasons, might have some dire consequences for my continued career.

In terms of planning for the future then, I really need to change tack. I can show how valuable I have been to the department in terms of the courses I have reorganized and taught, and I have student evaluations of teaching which show that I am doing a good job. But I think that I need to get going on research, or at least I need to confirm this in the appraisal interview. If, as I suspect, this is the case, then my immediate objectives are something like this:

- I will change the balance of my work to spend more time on research and publication.
- I will make a two-year action plan which will make sure that I have some publications and a research programme in place when I come up for tenure.
- I will talk this over in the appraisal interview, tell my HOD what I intend with regard to my action plan, and make sure that I am acting in my own best interests.

MICHAEL (MICHELLE) RICHARDS

Summary reminder. *Michael Richards is also a relatively new lecturer coming up for tenure. He has previous commercial and industrial experience but is enjoying the flexibility of an academic position. He has not had much to do with other people in the department. Michael has nearly completed a PhD; he published a couple of papers last year and has considerable PhD research material remaining. He has recently had a poor student evaluation of his teaching.*

In terms of my career long term, I want a reasonable salary but also the freedom to enjoy my family and children while they are still at home. When I worked in industry the salary was quite good and in fact I took a reduction to come into academia. However, I was having to travel and I was spending longer and longer periods away from home. I still put in a lot of hours as a lecturer but feel I have more control over what I do and when. So I'm quite happy with the nature of an academic job, and as far as I can see for the moment, I will stay where I am.

In the long term I am fairly ambitious and would not be happy if I stopped at the career grade. I may not make full prof, but I want to make reader or assoc. prof. With that kind of salary, maybe supplemented by some commercial consultation work later on, I think we would have a reasonable income and savings for retirement. It sounds awful to be looking that far ahead, but the family commitments especially have made me start to think in these terms.

In the short term there are two big things which I need to make sure happen. First, I need to finish my PhD and second, I need to have my appointment confirmed. I don't really see any problems with either. My PhD is all but finished already, and my supervisor has said ok to a complete first draft. Just a question of wading through, checking and tidying up. On the tenure side, I think I am doing ok and the only thing to have worried me was the poor teaching evaluation I had recently.

I don't really know if that matters or not. I can't believe that a student-based popularity contest could hold much weight. It still makes me feel bad though, and I would like to know where I stand on teaching. It's a shame that there is no one in the department I can talk to about it. I've tended to go in and teach and lock myself away in my office, and get home to the family as much as possible. I suppose if I had made more of an effort to meet and mix with people in the department it would be easier to ask for advice.

In terms of research I still have a mass of data from my PhD which I can mine for another year or two easily. The papers I produce from this will all be much of a muchness – not really progressing very far – so I want to start to develop away from my PhD topic. I might be able to work some of my former commercial contacts in here, and develop in a more applied way. There may be some research financing or consultation money in it too if I play my cards right. Taking everything into account then, the things I need to know and my immediate objectives are these:

- I will make sure that my interpretation of where I stand in terms of tenure (ie, that I am ok) is shared by the head of department. I need to know that I am ok on research, and I especially need to know if teaching is considered and if it is, how this is done and how important it is.

- Whether or not teaching is considered important for tenure, I want to find out why I got a poor evaluation, see if I should believe this result, and if so, do something about it. I will try to get to know one or two of my colleagues a bit better and ask their advice about this.

- I will clarify my objectives with regard to research, including finishing off my PhD, writing up papers, and looking to the future.

JANET (JOHN) SMITH

Summary reminder. Janet Smith has tenure and has published very successfully. She has had good student evaluations of her lectures, less so of her tutorials. She is very forceful in committee work. Janet is ambitious to advance and is frustrated that she is not advancing quickly enough. She is beginning to think about moving elsewhere.

I love the academic life and it is all I have ever wanted to do with my life. I had a mentor at university, the prof of my department, and I have wanted to be like her since my undergraduate days. She was decisive, creative, enthusiastic about teaching and enthusing students, enthusiastic about her research up to retirement and beyond, and *free* – I mean she always seemed to be able to determine what she wanted to do, and do it. She was a great role model for me and being something like her is how I see myself in the future. I want to be prof and head of department. I want to continue to establish an international reputation for myself, lead a strong department and play a role at an international level in my subject area.

I suppose that I have made a good start in my career but I am now getting very frustrated. People have said to me that I am in a hurry. It is true, that is exactly the way things are and at the moment I feel that I am losing time. To get where I intend I need rapid promotion, and that is not happening. I know all about the problems there are in the university regarding promotion, and that if I was in a different subject area then things would be different. None of that helps. I feel that I am stuck and time is passing me by. This has reached a point now where I think I should start looking for a change. I am not that committed to staying where I am, and would move at the drop of a hat to advance my career significantly. That may be overstating it a bit, but basically it is true.

My research is going well and I am well into a new book. I also have a good idea for the next major project after this one. Teaching is going well too. The evaluations I get are very good on the lecturing side, but I have had some negative response with regard to tutorials. In fact these responses have been rather like some of the comments colleagues have made about how I am in committees – maybe a bit forceful and dominating. I can see how this is counter-productive sometimes both in tutorials and in committees, but I don't see what I can do about it as it is simply the way I am. On reflection though, if I do see myself as a head of department in the future, I might *have* to learn some new skills in dealing with people. Thinking about it, my mentor was very good at this, and she always seemed to have time for people. Perhaps there is something I can do to change a little.

- I am clear where my career is going and it is becoming apparent to me that I may need to look at moving soon. I will discuss this with the HOD and listen to what he says.
- Unless the HOD comes up with something out of the blue, I think I will start looking more systematically in *The Times Higher* and *Campus News* for jobs. I will also start putting feelers out to my contacts about possible positions. I am giving a paper at an international conference soon and I will make it known to some of the people who will be there that I am dissatisfied where I am.
- Perhaps I could do something about the way I am with people – in the tutorials and committees, for example. Perhaps I could read a book or something. I will try to find out.

PAUL (PAULINE) WHITING

Summary reminder. Paul Whiting has been a lecturer for many years and has been at the career grade for a considerable time but has never applied for promotion beyond it. He has a grown-up family and no thoughts of leaving the university. He has not published anything recently despite having plenty of ideas. He is very committed to and enthusiastic about teaching although he has never taken a student evaluation of his teaching. The HOD has raised the possibility that he might take over some of the appraisal interviews in the department next year.

I am now 50. I am committed to this place and I don't want to move. Being realistic, I think it is unlikely that I will be promoted, and I am not really seeking promotion. I may take early retirement if I can afford to and there is a lot that I want to do when I retire. I have some strong interests outside of work and I have been thinking about how I could pursue some of these when I retire.

The real question for me is what my working life is going to be like from here until I retire, especially as it could still be some time until I go. I could carry on as normal with my teaching – I still enjoy teaching a lot. But my research has really fallen by the wayside over the years. Maybe I am getting sensitive in my old age but I feel that my standing in the department is not perhaps as high as it once was. I still get on very well with my colleagues and I am very interested in departmental affairs. But I feel that time is slipping by, and in a few years' time I can see how I might be pushed more and more to the margin, not really appreciated or valued any more. I definitely don't want that to happen.

As I see it I could concentrate my efforts in any of the areas of teaching, research or administration. I really like teaching but even after all of these years I *still* feel a bit of a novice. I'm sure there is more I could do to find out about my teaching – how it is going. Most of the comments I've had from students have been good, but I have had the odd comment which has been a bit negative. I suppose I could do something a bit more systematic to find out.

I am also interested in the students using computers themselves in some of my classes. It would be good if I could get this going and perhaps try to evaluate it. Maybe I could write it up as a paper? It would certainly be pretty different from the research I am used to, but it would be interesting to do. To be honest it would be very hard for me to get back into the research area in which I published in my early career. To be brutally honest I am not nearly so interested in it now anyway. I would be far more interested in something to do with the nitty-gritty of teaching, which is what I am involved in on a day-to-day basis. Introducing students to using computers in my classes would be really interesting.

I could also get more involved in the running of the department. The head has made some vague suggestions about this before. He says I am good at getting people to cooperate with each other and the meetings I run are productive, but also they have a nice atmosphere. He has hinted that I could take over some of the appraisal interviews next year. I think I might quite enjoy that, but I wouldn't have a clue where to start. I wonder why the head mentioned this to me; there are others who could do the job and who are senior to me. The headship is now 'revolving' for a fixed term, and not the strict territory of the profs any more. I know in other departments there are senior lecturers who are heads. It's a thought. I think I would be quite a popular choice. But would I want it? I guess that would depend. It would certainly be a new experience and make life interesting. I haven't really thought about it before, but I suppose it is a possibility.

- I am definitely going to get moving again, set some objectives and not just be a 'time server' until I retire.
- I will do something to find out about my teaching, how it is going and what I could do to improve it. I guess this means some kind of student evaluation of teaching.
- I will look into the computers idea with a view to making this into a research project too which I can write up for publication.
- I will talk to the HOD about the administrative role I play in the department and where he thinks I might make a contribution. I will find out a bit more about appraisal interviewing and what this would entail. When the opportunity arises, I will very cautiously and gently inquire how he sees the headship going in the next few years, and also keep my ears to the ground with respect to my colleagues.

CHARLES (CAROL) ROSS

Summary reminder. Charles Ross is professor and head of department. He is heavily involved in both departmental and university-level administration. Charles retains a fairly full teaching load, but has not published much over the last ten years. He has also lost contact with the international research organization on which he once served. He is contemplating the prospect of retirement in a few years' time.

The main thing on my mind now is obviously retirement. If I continue as I have been doing over the past few years, from now to retirement will consist mainly of spending large amounts of time serving on university and faculty committees, and administering the department. I will keep on with my usual teaching duties and not do any research. The trouble with all of this is that I want to maintain an active academic role after retirement, and I cannot see how continuing along these lines will make it possible.

I would like to be back in the position I was a few years ago. Then I was active in my subject area at national level, and was also quite heavily involved with the International Association. The reason I have lost contact in these areas over the past years is, I am convinced, because I stopped doing research. Before it is too late I want to get back into research, but I realize it will be difficult to pick up with the kind of research programme I was running years ago. I still feel that I could do something, however, perhaps something in the way of strategic planning – looking at priorities for research and research funding in my area. I could put my committee skills to good use in this area too if the chance presented itself.

I have little time left to make a change in direction. Almost certainly I will need to think again about the responsibilities I am carrying at the moment, and redistributing these. I think I should keep on my teaching, and so still be seen to be pulling my weight in the department. However, I could perhaps accelerate the process of changeover of the headship. Instead of thinking in terms of three years down the track, there is really no reason why this could not take place in a little over a year's time. I know I will find it difficult to hand over control as I have been so used to being in charge, and I enjoy it. That is probably why I have been putting off thinking about handing over, but really to make a change of direction in terms of my career, it is probably necessary. It would also be nice to have a block of time available to help me get on with my plans geared towards strategic planning and research priorities. I wonder if I could arrange this? All in all, then, my objectives seem to be as follows:

- I need to re-establish contact with people at both the national and international levels. I will put some thought into this: who, how and when.
- I will talk to the dean about gradually relinquishing some of my faculty and university committee work. I could afford to keep up some of this work, especially the committees which hold out the prospect of national involvement in areas of university management, research and strategic planning. That fits in with my plan to place myself in a position where I can play a continuing role after retirement.
- I will offer to keep on the teaching responsibilities that I presently have within the department if that is agreeable when we discuss who is doing what. I cannot see people wanting to take over my courses, so I think my colleagues will be happy for me to keep on teaching them.
- I will start the process of handing over the headship. There is a lot I can do to ease this process and I will start it straight away. If all goes well, I could relinquish control in a little over a year's time.
- By the time I hand over the headship I should also have disengaged myself from most of the faculty and university committees I want to drop off. This would then present an opportune time to take some leave and get my teeth into the research on strategic planning and research funding, and perhaps do some travelling to re-establish contact with colleagues abroad. I will try to negotiate this with the dean. I think he will be sympathetic, but if all else fails I could ask for unpaid leave.

Your own career plan

These then are some attempts made by academics at differing career positions, to state where their careers stand at the moment, and where they are going in the future. You may have noticed that the plans produced are not very formal, that some of the things which appear as objectives are not really objectives at all, and that very little detail is given about exactly *how* the objectives are to be accomplished. At this stage, none of this matters. The point is that the people in the cases are attempting to put into their own words what they see as their *long-term* career objectives, and then to work out the consequences which follow for their shorter-term actions.

This is what you should now attempt. Again, it is important that you *write down* your observations, thoughts, interpretations and objectives as you consider the questions which follow. Do not be concerned at this point to go into too much detail. In later chapters you will have the opportunity to plan in more detail your objectives in the specific areas of teaching, research and other responsibilities. For the moment, it is long-term career objectives you are considering, and then *general* short-term objectives and priorities.

- *Where do you see your career going? What do you want to accomplish?*
- *Try to visualize and describe how you see yourself on the day you retire. What career point have you reached? What happened in your career?*
- *Turn the question around. What career point would you be **disappointed** to have reached when you retire? Explain why you think this way.*
- *How important are the following to you and can you place them in order of priority?*
  - *Promotion, even if it means moving elsewhere.*
  - *Remaining at your present institution.*
  - *Teaching the subjects you are teaching presently.*
  - *Teaching new or different courses in which you are interested.*
  - *Having more time (better facilities, more money, etc) to pursue research.*
  - *Remaining in your present locality, region, country.*
  - *Other personal circumstances, eg, being near parents, relatives or friends, your spouse's job, children's schooling, hobbies, etc.*
- *Without becoming too specific and without saying exactly **how** you would accomplish them, what **general** objectives do you think are important for you in order to develop your career? You might consider this question with respect to both the long term (anything from 10 years up to retirement) and the short term (one to two years). You might also think in terms of the main categories of your work (eg, teaching, supervision, research, research funding, administration, consultation, clinical responsibility, etc) and the balance you see between these.*
- *How can you bring the insights you may have developed in working through this chapter into your next appraisal interview? How far do you wish to reveal your long-term plans in an appraisal interview? How far do the short-term plans and activities you may have outlined in a previous appraisal interview make sense when seen in terms of the longer-term perspective you have just considered?*

Chapter Four

Where am I now with my teaching?

Introduction

Having considered your career generally, we now come down to what for most of us is a very important aspect of our careers: our teaching. In this chapter we will look at the evaluation of teaching, and how you can try to determine where you stand, or 'Where am I now?', with regard to your teaching. This leads on to the next chapter where we will consider how you can go about deciding what plans you want to make and what you wish to achieve in your teaching.

As a lecturer you constantly receive information about your teaching. Students come up to you after a lecture to say that they enjoyed it, that they could not see what was at the bottom of an overhead transparency, or that they missed the last point because you were going too fast. Students in your tutorial group show that they have misunderstood a point which you thought you had more than adequately covered in your last lecture. Others tell you that they were interested and found a good paper on the subject in the library. A test or examination reveals widespread misunderstanding of a point which you covered in a lecture. Your third-year class is large this year with many choosing to take it after hearing favourable reports from last year's group. A colleague says that he has heard how well your course is going this year. The head of department warns you that she has heard rumblings about your first-year practical class. Be it informal, anecdotal, guileful, well intentioned, misconceived or misconstrued, your teaching *is* being talked about and evaluated.

This is as it should be. As lecturers we are paid to teach, and it is reasonable to expect that we should be accountable for this activity. But more than that, it is also *personally* important to us. We want to know that we are teaching at least adequately, better still that we are teaching well. If we have fears or doubts concerning our teaching, these can sour our professional lives, our relationships with students, our own self-esteem. The question, 'Where am I now with my teaching?' is so fundamental that it seems inconceivable that lecturers would *not* want to evaluate their teaching. However, many and varied reasons have been put forward for not doing so and these need to be faced squarely before we can proceed.

Can teaching be evaluated?

The discussion immediately above suggests that teaching is constantly being evaluated whether or not the lecturer has anything to do with it. The problem with information coming from sources such as those noted above is that it does not necessarily provide an *adequate* evaluation of teaching. *Any* form of information relating to your teaching is potentially interesting and useful. The question remains, however, whether teaching can systematically be evaluated in such a way that we can have confidence in the information which is provided. This is especially true with regard to *student evaluation of teaching*, which is the most important and controversial area of teaching evaluation.

Student evaluation of teaching

Happily there is a wealth of empirical evidence from many hundreds of academic papers written on the subject of student evaluation of teaching.[1] We will briefly consider some of the arguments raised against student evaluation of teaching, and some of the evidence. Gus Pennington (1992) considers seven common misconceptions about evaluations of teaching (outlined below) and to these we may add a few more.

Teaching is an art which cannot or should not be measured

This argument can be made with respect to any kind of teaching evaluation, but it seems particularly common when student evaluation of teaching is proposed. Personally, I have no doubt that teaching, like most other professional practices, is a subtle and highly complex activity. Reducing it to a single number can devalue this subtlety and complexity. On the other hand, Pennington argues that, 'effective teaching consists of a set of relatively ordinary and teachable behaviours which can be improved through training and practice' (p. 64). I partly agree with that too. Teaching can be analysed, we can find out what is working in a given context and lecturers can learn how to teach differently, how to change. Analysis, reduction and simplification demonstrate a 'scientific' approach to the problem whereas a holistic blending together of the teacher's knowledge, experience and 'being', within a given teaching context, is an essentially 'artistic' endeavour. There is room for both in the development of our teaching.

The real problem with a point blank refusal to consider teaching evaluation is that it leads nowhere. How can we learn about our teaching, how can we decide what to do in order to improve it? Whatever means we use to evaluate teaching will never capture the complexity of the activity in its entirety. But this is no argument against learning what we can about our teaching. It should not prevent us from benefiting from the insights and understandings we can gain from teaching evaluation.

You can never please students

In many student evaluations of teaching there are responses throughout the range from very good to very bad. Some students will tend to prefer one approach to teaching and learning, while others prefer a different approach. On average, however, students tend to be rather generous in their ratings of lecturers. Marsh (1987) found this to be the case in his review, and it has also been the experience of the University of Otago system (described later in this section) where, on average, students describe their teachers as 'effective'.

It is also worth noting that *student* characteristics such as age, sex, level, personality and grade point average are not related to the ratings which students give to their teachers (Cashin, 1990).

Student ratings have more to do with a teacher's popularity and personality than with effectiveness

This is a common belief among lecturers but the research evidence contradicts it. Measures of popularity and personality do not correlate significantly with student evaluations of teaching (Marsh, 1987). A nice person might also be a good teacher, but students do not confuse these two things. Other *teacher* variables which show little or no relationship with student ratings are: sex, age, teaching experience and research productivity (Cashin, 1990).

Student ratings reflect entertainment value rather than substance

This is a related point which gained credence with the 'Dr Fox' experiment in the early 1970s. 'Dr Fox' along with many others addressed a medical conference for a very short time. 'Dr Fox' was rated most favourably because of the interesting, enthusiastic and expressive manner he used. 'Dr Fox' was in fact a professional actor, who knew nothing of substance about his topic (Naftulin *et al*, 1973). However, in the ensuing argument over this case, it was agreed by all (including the authors) that the 'experiment' had serious flaws, the main one being that the audience received the lecture in a context which was quite different to the normal educational context. That is, they were not expected to learn any specific content from the lecture and they did not need to learn anything which would be required subsequently in testing or evaluation.

When the experiment was repeated under normal classroom conditions (ie, students realized that they needed to learn in order to progress, and instruction continued for a long period, not just a few minutes), the 'Dr Fox' effect was not replicated (Marsh, 1987). A teacher's expressiveness and enthusiasm *are* related to successful learning and thus to positive student evaluations of teaching. However, under normal classroom and lecture theatre conditions, entertainment cannot *replace* substance in securing good student evaluations of teaching.

It is much easier to get a good rating from a small class

Not true. Many studies have shown that correlations between class size and student ratings are very low (Cashin, 1990; Marsh, 1987).

Easy courses and lenient marking ensure good student evaluations

Not true on either count. The evidence suggests that easy grading has no positive effect on student ratings, and that if anything, higher ratings are associated with a rigorous and demanding workload (Marsh, 1987; Pennington, 1992).

Students realize the value of the course only after they have left

Possibly true. Students can come to appreciate the value of a *course* at a later date. But their ratings of the *teacher* do *not* change. Student ratings of teaching are remarkably reliable and have long-term stability (Marsh, 1987).

Students rate traditional courses higher than innovative ones

I have heard this argument used by lecturers to explain their poor student evaluations on courses which they consider to be outside the norm, or innovatory. I do not know of any systematic research which has considered this criticism. From our own experience at Otago, however, innovatory courses involving problem-based, case-based and self-directed methods have been found among the highest rated courses of all, and alongside large, conventional lecture classes.

Students lack maturity

Teachers who have taken student evaluations of their classes sometimes get irrelevant comments concerning such things as their choice of clothing or hair style. The argument goes that because of this, students lack the necessary maturity for evaluating teaching. Scriven (1988, p. 10) notes how lecturers may be happy to quote the views of their own children concerning a teacher, while at the same time being against student evaluation of

teaching. He further notes how discussions at senate sometimes leave much
to be desired in terms of evaluative maturity. In an evaluation which a head
of department made of his performance and which I helped to administer,
one lecturer commented in a section concerned with areas for improvement:
'Needs to work on his backhand at squash'. The head of department did not
consider that this comment negated the evaluation which followed.

I would argue that the presence of irrelevant comment does not invalidate
an overall class evaluation. The vast majority of students take the exercise
seriously and the demonstrated reliability of the results suggests that their
evaluations are far from being based on whim.

So what are student ratings associated with?

Student evaluations of teaching *are* significantly related to the teacher's own
self-evaluations. Most important of all, they are related to learning. Students
perform better (according to test or examination results set and marked
independently by others) on courses where they award teachers high
ratings (Marsh, 1987).

> . . . classes in which the students gave the instructor higher ratings tend to be the
> classes where the students learned more, ie scored higher on the external exam
> (Cashin, 1990, p. 3).

Or to put it another way:

> It is surely from the privileged position of the students in reporting on how well
> the instructor has explained the subject matter to them, and the centrality of that
> consideration in their overall rating, that the high positive correlation with
> learning gains emerges (Scriven, 1988, p. 12).

Cohen's (1981) meta-analysis of 41 independent validity studies (representing 68 separate multisection courses) also confirmed the relationship
between student ratings and student achievement (the overall correlation
was 0.43). This led Cohen to conclude that: 'the results . . . provide strong
support for the validity of student ratings as measures of teaching
effectiveness' (p. 281).

Alternatives for evaluating teaching

Visitors

One possible alternative to student evaluation of teaching is for peers,
colleagues, staff developers, administrators or outside 'inspectors' to attend
a teacher's classes and evaluate them. The research suggests that such
sources provide information which is less sensitive, reliable and valid than
are student ratings and that it does not correspond very closely with student
or self-evaluation (Marsh, 1987). Scriven (1988) in particular has been
scathing on the use of visitors for teaching evaluation. The two crucial points
he makes are:

- the time visitors typically spend in the classroom dismally fails to provide for adequate sampling;
- visitors lack the crucial cognitive qualifications to judge the adequacy of explanations. In short, they are not at the same level or in the same position as students and it is the students' understandings which are important.

Colleagues may be able to reflect back to a teacher some of the things which he or she did in a lecture and may be able to offer advice or suggestions. Staff developers may also do this. Colleagues and others can certainly offer a different perspective. But whatever the qualifications of visitors, their views cannot compare in importance with the views of those most intimately involved in the learning process: the students themselves. There are also some dangers in that visitors may simply speak from their own preferences and prejudices. The fact that another teacher approaches teaching in a different manner from oneself does not necessarily make either approach 'wrong', only different. Because they are not intimately involved in grappling with, assimilating and learning new material, visitors may also tend to concentrate on 'style' rather than overall effectiveness.

An aspect of teaching in which a colleague *can* have a more legitimate role is that of providing feedback on the *level* or currency of course materials and assessments. The argument can be made that whereas students provide the most valid source as to the effectiveness of teaching, they are not so well placed to comment on the standard or level of a course. This is a contentious argument, but certainly a colleague can add to the information which a teacher may collect on his or her teaching with regard to the standard, level or currency of a course.

Students' results

Can teaching be evaluated from the results obtained by students? To some extent teachers *are* judged in this way, usually collectively, in terms of the reputation of an institution. There are some problems here, however, most notably what Scriven (1988) describes as the 'Harvard fallacy', which is:

> . . . the fallacy of supposing that the teaching at Harvard must be good because its graduates do very well in later life . . . All that one can infer from that data is that Harvard does not inflict permanent brain damage – *usually*. The rest of the trick lies in selecting a talented student entering class and not getting in the way of their use of the library, labs, peer tutoring, and family influence or brand-name reverence. The contribution from the faculty, if any, is the residue after factoring out . . . the effect of the 'old boys' network' and brand recognition, on job selection and promotion. While Harvard is demonstrably a great university, it is certainly not demonstrably a great teaching university, just a superbly equipped one' (p. 17).

Universities in other countries can obviously be substituted for Harvard. But even if it were possible to compare results from similar courses at similar institutions, Scriven's point about attributing success to teaching as opposed to other factors would still remain. Even some form of 'value added' measurement would not get around this, and such measurements could either be so crude as to be meaningless, or so complex that an unreasonable amount of time would be needed for testing and measurement in comparison with the supposedly central activities of teaching and learning. Comparing results within the same institution from one year to the next also raises problems concerning changing circumstances within departments and in the student population.

Self-evaluation

Self-evaluation is of central importance for teachers in trying to work out whether they are achieving what they intend, what they think is going well, what is not going so well and in what areas they see a need for change. For *developmental* purposes, self-evaluation is vital and we will consider it later in this chapter.

We have already seen that the results of self-evaluation also tend to correspond quite well with results from student evaluations of teaching. Despite this, the main problem with self-evaluation is that the validity of the results is often questioned by others. This is particularly true if you wish to evaluate your teaching in order to make a case for tenure or promotion. I will call this the use of teaching evaluation for *institutional* purposes. Heads of departments and promotions committees tend to be persuaded by what they see as more 'objective' evidence from sources such as student evaluations or visitors. The role of self-evaluation in these circumstances thus tends to be seen as a corroborative one.

Course and departmental evaluation

Teaching need not be evaluated solely at the level of the individual teacher. A teacher's course may be evaluated instead of the teacher him or herself. These are not the same things, however. Students may see that a course is valuable, but be very disappointed in the teaching they receive.

A number of lecturers teaching a course may choose to evaluate the course as a whole rather than their own sections of the course. This can reveal interesting information about the course and what parts of it were particularly valued or found wanting. Similarly in departmental reviews, there is the opportunity for the lecturer's teaching to be viewed in the wider context of the department's offerings as a whole. Evaluations taken of teaching at both the course and departmental levels can add valuable information. The problem is once more that for *institutional* purposes, you will almost certainly need to make a case concerning your own teaching. Course or departmental evaluation information, like self-evaluation, can play a part in this but, rightly or wrongly, it will often be a corroborative part.

Summary

The discussion above has been quite long in order to deal with some of the popular misconceptions concerning student evaluation of teaching. The position I have taken is that *any* source of information on your teaching is potentially useful and that using a number of means of evaluation can help you to gain a more accurate overall picture of your teaching. Among the sources, however, student evaluation of teaching is central and provides the single most important insight.

How can I evaluate my teaching ?[2]

The first question you need to consider with regard to evaluating your own teaching is: what is the purpose of the evaluation? The two most common purposes are those which were outlined above, namely for *institutional* reasons (to help make a case for tenure or promotion) and for *developmental* reasons (to help you improve your teaching). These are not necessarily mutually exclusive. In fact, during an appraisal interview both may be on the agenda, and may be conflated. It will help clarify matters, however, if we start off by treating them independently.

Evaluating teaching for institutional purposes

You need to check whether your institution, faculty or department has a standard system and form for teaching evaluation. The staff or educational development unit should be able to help you here, or in developing a form if none exists. Remember that the requirements for an institutional form can be rather different from those of a form to help you develop your teaching. In all probability, you will not gain a great deal of information to help you decide in what ways you should develop your teaching from a standard institutional form.

To be useful for an institution in gauging your case for tenure or promotion, an evaluation of teaching form needs to be *standard* in order that comparisons can be made across the institution. It also needs to be *simple* in order to assist processing and prevent student resistance. It should not be biased towards particular teaching approaches, behaviours or styles.

The best way for a student evaluation of teaching scheme to be developed is with the cooperation and participation of staff throughout the institution. During the process of consultation and development of an institutional scheme, vastly different perspectives and contexts from throughout the institution will be put forward. Institutions themselves also vary markedly in their character and requirements. This having been said, there is usually a fair degree of similarity in the schemes and forms which are produced.

An example of a standard student evaluation of teaching form for institutional purposes is given in Appendix I. This form, together with the form for peer evaluation and items for obtaining feedback from students were developed by Dr Terry Crooks for the University of Otago. They have been in use there for some time and have also been adopted by other institutions (universities and polytechnics) in a number of other countries. If your institution does not have a standard form for evaluating teaching for institutional purposes, you might consider using this one.

Administering the form

- Choose a class session in which you expect attendance to be at least average, but not one involving a test or other stressful activity.
- Allow ten minutes at the end of a class for the questionnaire to be distributed, filled in, and collected.
- Tell the students that you would like their comments on your teaching. If you have only taught part of the course, clarify that they are asked to comment on *your* teaching only.
- Ask one particular student (eg, a class representative) to collect the completed questionnaires and take them to the place where you have arranged to have them processed. The educational or staff development unit may be able to provide processing for you.
- Distribute the questionnaires and leave the room.

Interpretation of results from a student evaluation of teaching

In Appendix II (p 136) some instructions are given on how to calculate results for a student evaluation of teaching exercise. This is followed in Appendix III (p 138) by an example of results obtained from such an exercise. How can these results be interpreted?

The questionnaire was designed following Scriven's (1981) suggestions. The idea is that students focus first on their perceptions of and responses to the course and then on some specific attributes of the teacher and teaching which have repeatedly been found to be highly related to an overall rating of the teaching. As you can see from Appendices II and III these are:

- communication of ideas and information;
- stimulation of interest;
- attitude toward students.

All of this is by way of preparation for question six, which is a global question concerning how effective students have found the teaching to be overall. The result from question six is the main item of interest to promotion committees.

In the example given, Dr Garwood scored 1.72 on question six. To put this into context, the average score from over 2,000 classes analysed at the University of Otago over the past five years has consistently been around 2.00 (or 'effective'). In other words, 50 per cent of the classes analysed would be evaluated as better than 2.00 (ie, from 1–1.99) and 50 per cent would be worse than 2.00 (ie 2–5). Dr Garwood's result thus places her as above average (in fact in the top 33 per cent of teachers at Otago). The standard deviation indicated in the results gives a measurement of the spread of responses. A standard deviation of 1.00 or above suggests a fairly wide spread of response, and this can be seen from Dr Garwood's results, with students having made use of four out of the five possible categories of the scale.

We could also imagine the scores which some of the people in the case studies introduced earlier might have obtained. For example, Janet (John) Smith had received good evaluations of her lecturing (perhaps a score of 1.5, placing her in about the top 20 per cent of classes evaluated) while Michael (Michelle) Richards had received a poor evaluation about which he was quite worried. If Michael's score had been 3.0 for example, his worries would be well founded, as this would place him in the bottom 7 per cent of classes evaluated.

Can the norms from Otago be used to interpret your own results if you use this method? No definitive answer can be given to this question as it depends on how different your own context is. However, there is no reason to suppose that Otago represents an extraordinarily special case. Otago is a medium-sized university with 12,000 full-time students and a normal range of subjects grouped into humanities, sciences, commerce and health sciences. The fact that other institutions have adopted the Otago scheme, and that many others have produced very similar schemes themselves, also argues in favour of generalizability.

About 60 per cent of staff at Otago use this system of teaching evaluation. This percentage almost certainly constitutes a greater proportion of more highly rated teachers, and fewer lowly rated teachers, than would be found in the university population as a whole. For example, the median for question six (the global question concerning the overall effectiveness of the teacher) is actually 1.95 for the 60 per cent of staff who use this evaluation system. If all academic staff in the university used the system it would probably be about 2.15 (ie, 0.2 added on). We have allowed for this in defining three broad bands which can be used to interpret the results from question six, as follows:

1.00–1.75   Distinctly positive, above average (top 37 per cent)
1.76–2.75   Positive to equivocal (middle 53 per cent)
2.76–5.00   Equivocal to very negative, below average (bottom 10 per cent).

So, you can certainly use this information to see where you would stand if you were a teacher at Otago. Unless your own context is very different from that described, there is no reason why you should not use these broad bandings in order to obtain at least a preliminary idea of where you stand presently with regard to your teaching.

Peer evaluation

As explained earlier, comments from a colleague concerning your teaching may legitimately be used for institutional purposes especially with regard to the standard, level and currency of the courses you teach. Such comments can be used to corroborate the results from student evaluation of teaching, as can comments from other sources such as an external examiner. Appendix IV (p 140) contains a standard form for eliciting comments from a colleague on your teaching.

Teaching portfolio

I have argued that student evaluation is vital in documenting your teaching for institutional purposes. Peer evaluation can also be used in order to gain another perspective. However, if your institution allows you to provide a fuller picture of your teaching activities, to be taken into account for tenure or promotion, then you might want to produce a teaching portfolio.

Details of how to produce a teaching portfolio are covered in Gibbs (1989), Canadian Association of University Teachers (1978) and O'Neil and Pennington (1992). A portfolio to be used for institutional purposes is best kept short and pithy, with an emphasis on evidence and example. Based upon the sources noted, here are some general areas which you might consider in producing a teaching portfolio:

- What are you aiming for in your teaching; what is your educational philosophy; how has this changed and developed; how can you illustrate this?
- How do you teach; what innovative approaches have you introduced and why; what special teaching skills have you developed; what course materials have you produced; what course design or course development work have you initiated or contributed to?
- What levels and abilities of students have you taught; can you show how you have coped with students of differing background, ability or motivation; how do you assist students who are struggling or stimulate those who are coping with ease?
- What assessment strategies do you use; have you introduced any innovations such as self- or peer assessment; how do you provide feedback for improving learning; how can you demonstrate successful student learning and achievement?
- How do you review and evaluate your teaching; how have you acted on this information to change and develop your teaching?
- What teaching qualifications, distinctions or awards do you have? What courses, conferences, seminars and workshops on teaching have you attended? Do you belong to a teaching-related association? Have you researched, published or presented at a conference anything relating to teaching? Have you received any teaching development or similar grants? Do you regularly read teaching-related journals or other literature?

- Have you contributed towards the professional development of colleagues within the institution or elsewhere; what coordinating or leadership roles in teaching have you taken; how have you contributed to the development of teaching in your institution?

Evaluating teaching for developmental purposes

Student questionnaires

In comparison with standard forms of student evaluation for institutional purposes, student questionnaires which are intended to provide feedback for *developmental* purposes can be far more flexible. There is no need for standardization, indeed you will wish to search out useful information concerning your own particular and idiosyncratic circumstances. But although there is no need to use a standard (and short) form, there is still good reason for using scaled response (eg, choose a number between 1 and 5), as this will allow you to cover the full breadth of what you do in your teaching without undue burden being placed upon students. This time, however, it is up to you to decide what it is you want to find out about.

For guidance, a large number of questions have been supplied in Appendix V (p 142). These have again been taken from the Otago system developed by Terry Crooks to provide lecturers with an easy and accessible way in which to obtain useful feedback from students. Calculation of results can be undertaken as outlined in Appendix II.

Before you select items from this list, or construct your own items, please read the rest of this section. It is important that you select not only issues which are of interest to you, but ones which are of importance to students as well. It is also a good idea to include open-ended response. These concerns are considered below.

Open-ended response

So far in this section, lecturers have determined what they feel it is important to find out or know about their teaching. This is obviously lopsided, for the lecturer's view of what is important may not be that of the students. It is imperative that students are given the opportunity to indicate what *they* think is important about your teaching, and the easiest way in which this can be accomplished is to provide space for open-ended response. Such response can also be a useful way of establishing specific issues for closed items in a future survey.

A popular way of providing for open-ended comment is to pose the following three questions, leaving a blank space under each, in which students can write:

- What were the best aspects of this course and my teaching of it; what did you most enjoy?

- What changes would you most like to see in the course and my teaching of it? (Please try to be specific.)
- Do you have any other comments?

When you receive the responses, read them all through so as to gain an overall impression and then return to the first one. Read the response to the first question and try to organize what has been said into a few category headings. Move on to the next student's response to that question and make tally marks if similar things are being said under the categories you already have, or add more categories. After working your way through the pile you should have a good idea of the frequency with which particular points are being made, and thus what the *students* feel to be their main concerns.

Interviews and discussions

Interviews and discussions with either individuals or small groups of students from your course can be helpful. Throughout the normal running of the course, opportunities for this may present themselves: take advantage of these and make a note of issues which are raised. You may wish to call together a small group of students *before* drawing up a questionnaire to go to the whole class, in an attempt to make sure that matters which are of concern to students are raised on the questionnaire. When the results come in you will see how widespread the concerns of the small group of students were for the class as a whole.

Interviews and discussions can also be useful *after* you have received feedback from a questionnaire. Providing it is possible to get a group of students together at this time, you can use the opportunity to delve further into the reasons for the responses you received from the questionnaire.

For example, many students may have indicated on the questionnaire that they thought too much was crammed into the course. In an informal interview you could try to find out more about this. Was it, for example, the case throughout the course or just in the last few weeks? Did the exercises or assessments you set come at the same time as other assignments and thus put students under pressure? Were material resources such as references in the library or access to labs adequate? What more could you have done to help? What do they think was peripheral in the material you covered, what could be cut down or dropped? What did they see as being central and crucial?

During a discussion session, whether it is held before or after you carry out a questionnaire exercise, try to encourage the students to talk and do not attempt to rationalize and justify everything you did. By all means ask for clarification or examples, and test whether a particular person's opinion is generally held. Remember, however, that this is an opportunity for the students to speak and for you to learn what *their* experience was. You may disagree with some of what the students say, but when it comes to planning the course for next year, you will be in a better position to make informed choices.

Gibbs *et al.* (1989) counsel against using *unstructured* meetings of the whole group in attempting to obtain useful feedback. It is likely that most of the students will not contribute and that extreme and strongly held views will dominate. This has been my experience too, so if you do want to hold a whole group session (or part of a session) in order to obtain feedback, try the procedure Gibbs *et al.* (1989) recommend for *structured* group feedback (pp. 69–71).

A slightly modified form of this would involve students working individually to identify what they considered to be the best aspects of the course, what aspects could have been improved and how. They consider this in terms of the course, the teaching and themselves (the students). They then form groups of four to discuss their views, but record only those comments on which a majority can agree. The teacher (or a colleague) then takes a point concerning what was good about the course from a group and asks if most of the other groups agree with this. If so, it is recorded on a board or OHP. After finishing good points to do with the course, ways in which it could have been improved are then considered. This process is then repeated for the teaching of the course, and the students (see Gibbs *et al.*, 1989).

Self-evaluation

Most of us come out of a teaching session with an impression of how well it went, what mistakes we made and possibly some ideas concerning what we would do differently next time. Sometimes we make short notes with the intention of using these in a future session. But often the pressure of other things which need to be attended to urgently means that we never get round to seriously considering the thoughts we have had. Not until next year, that is, when the experience of *déjà vu* can be quite disconcerting.

Some teachers keep a log book of the most important experiences they have had in teaching during the day. This may be organized in a number of ways, but one is to have different sections devoted to activities such as: lecturing, tutorials, practicals, marking essays, etc. If you wish to experiment with this idea, you may want to make a brief note of the class or context, what you did, what happened, your interpretation of this and your thoughts on what you would do next time.

You might also want quickly to assess how well you felt the class went according to criteria which you think are important. A short general checklist of criteria might look something like the one shown in Figure 4.1.

Figure 4.1 *A short checklist of criteria for self-evaluation*

How successfully did I:	Very successfully	Moderately successfully	Rather unsuccessfully
1 Prepare myself and my materials for the session			
2 Introduce the session and make the aims clear			
3 Organize the content			
4 Vary the process (eg, by using visual aids, providing for discussion, etc)			
5 Win and maintain student interest			
6 Convey an encouraging, positive and helpful attitude towards students			
7 Show my own enthusiasm for the subject			

The same checklist can be used at the end of a course to assist your reflections and self-evaluation of how your teaching of the course as a whole has gone this year, and for thinking about what changes you might wish to make for next year.

Mixed-purpose evaluation and evaluation for appraisal

Thus far I have kept evaluation for institutional and for developmental purposes separate. There are good reasons for doing this in order that confusion over purpose does not spread into the evaluation methods used. However, in the process of institutional *appraisal* (ie, your appraisal interview) this distinction may become blurred. You may find yourself talking about how your teaching has been going, plans for your teaching in the future, the importance of teaching in promotional decision-making and evidence you can submit to a promotions committee concerning your teaching. The discussion of your teaching may be wide ranging, rather than sharply focused. Also you may find it either necessary or convenient to collect information concerning your teaching for *both* institutional and developmental purposes at the same time. For this reason, we now consider how you might go about producing information for both purposes concurrently.

The first point to note is that even an evaluation questionnaire devised solely for institutional purposes, such as that given in Appendix I, also contains information which can be of developmental use. For example, questions 2, 3, 4 and 5 yield information on some of the criteria which have been found repeatedly to be highly related to question six: the overall effectiveness of the teacher. The correlations between each of these aspects of teaching and question six, according to the Otago experience, are as follows:

- question 2: course organization and effectiveness: 0.81
- question 3: ability to communicate ideas and information: 0.93
- question 4: stimulation of interest: 0.85
- question 5: attitude towards students: 0.74.

These are very high correlations indeed, and emphasize the degree to which each of these factors is associated with the students' overall rating of teaching. The norms for each question can be of use too.

Question	Top 10%	Top 25%	50%	Low 25%	Low 10%
1	1.67	2.00	2.28	2.65	2.89
2	1.29	1.47	1.84	2.09	2.47
3	1.39	1.67	2.02	2.55	3.17
4	1.61	1.93	2.32	2.81	3.15
5	1.10	1.30	1.50	1.88	2.17
6	1.37	1.62	1.95	2.31	2.75

A note of caution needs to be expressed once more in that these norms almost certainly refer to a sample containing more highly rated teachers than would be found in the university population as a whole. Again, a reasonable estimate of medians for the university population as a whole would require adding 0.2 to the sample medians (eg, the median of 1.95 on question six for this 60 per cent sample would be about 2.15 for the university population as a whole).

It is possible to use such information to judge where you presently stand with respect to these important criteria of teaching effectiveness. For illustration, we could look at a hypothetical example from the case studies introduced earlier.

We know that Michael (Michelle) Richards has received a poor student evaluation of teaching about which he is concerned. We know too that his score on question six put him in the bottom seven per cent of classes to have been analysed. But where does the problem lie? Suppose that Michael's scores on the other questions were as follows:

1. value of the course: 2.35   (45th percentile)
2. organization: 1.85   (50th percentile)
3. communication of ideas and information: 2.40   (30th percentile)
4. stimulation of interest: 4.30   (1st percentile)
5. attitude toward students: 2.00   (16th percentile)

Looking at these scores in terms of the norms given above, we see that the students viewed the course as being of about average value (45th percentile) and rated Michael's organization as average (50th percentile). You may remember that Michael talked about spending a lot of time preparing materials for his class, which ties in with his score on organization. His ability to communicate ideas and information was rated as below average and in the bottom 30 per cent (30th percentile). However, when it came to stimulation of interest, Michael scored very poorly indeed by being in the bottom one per cent (1st percentile). His attitude to students was also rated quite low, placing him in the bottom 16 per cent on this item.

Here then is a clear indication of where some of Michael's problems lie, and what he needs to do in order to improve his overall evaluation. It seems that he should present his (quite well organized) material in more interesting ways, perhaps trying to capture the students' imagination more, to show the relevance of the subject and to find ways of conveying his own interest and enthusiasm more clearly. He could also think about the way in which his attitude to students comes across in the lecture theatre.

A mixed questionnaire

So useful *developmental* information *can* come from a questionnaire designed for institutional purposes. Developmentally-oriented questions can also be added to such a questionnaire and there are good reasons for doing this.

It is a simple matter to add to the short evaluation questionnaire (Appendix I) a number of specific questions in which you are interested, perhaps taking these from Appendix V. Open-ended questions such as those outlined above can also be included, perhaps on the back of the sheet. The main problems to be avoided in using a mixed questionnaire of this type are those of confusion over what information is to be used for what purpose, and the tendency to ask too many questions (thus making the questionnaire unnecessarily burdensome for students).

By way of a guide, if you choose to use the six questions in Appendix I then perhaps a maximum of ten further rating type questions from Appendix V could also be included, plus two or three open-ended questions. You will need to allow at least 15 minutes at the end of a class for the completion and collection of forms. To ensure a good return rate, it is far better to set this time aside than to distribute the forms at the very end of the class and ask for them to be handed in at a later date.

The information you receive from such a questionnaire should prove useful for the institutional appraisal interview. Not only will you have an evaluation of how your teaching is regarded by students (Appendix I items) which you may be able to use for tenure or promotion purposes, but you will also have responses regarding some of the areas which you want to know more about and, from the open-ended questions, some idea of the areas which students feel are important. This information can help you developmentally in planning changes to your teaching for next year, which you can consider in the 'forward looking' part of the appraisal interview.

WHERE AM I NOW WITH MY TEACHING? 59

Now it's your turn

- *Where do I stand with regard to evaluating my teaching? What evidence do I have concerning my teaching?*

These are the key questions of this chapter. You may be able to answer them fully already. On the other hand you may have no systematic evidence at present. If the latter, this does not mean that you should try to find out everything about every course you teach and every teaching method you use, all in one go. You can plan a strategy over a number of years, and more is said about this in the next chapter. However, the following questions may provide a useful framework within which to consider where you presently stand with regard to your teaching.

- *How do I see myself as a teacher?*

What do you see as being your strengths as a teacher; what do you think you do particularly well and what do you enjoy doing? What things about teaching do you not enjoy; what areas do you think you need to improve in? What changes have you already made with regard to your teaching? Do you think that you are becoming a better teacher – how do you know?

- *What evidence or information will my institution allow me to present for decision-making purposes such as tenure or promotion?*

It is vital that if you do not already know this, you find out as quickly as possible. Is there a standard teaching evaluation form and if not, can you use a form such as that provided in Appendix I, or submit a teaching portfolio? Similarly, what information on teaching is required for the appraisal interview? For appraisal, you may well need to provide information concerning your teaching which is both evaluative (backward looking) and developmental (forward looking – in what ways you intend to change your teaching and why). Can you do this?

In order to meet these requirements the sections we have considered above on the evaluation of teaching for institutional purposes *and* for developmental purposes, should provide a good start. A mixed form of questionnaire may fit the bill by allowing you to collect evidence for both purposes at the same time. You may also wish to consider self- and peer evaluation, as outlined above, for contributing further useful information.

- *Where do I stand with regard to evaluating my (second-year) course?*

If you want to evaluate the teaching of a specific course, you might begin by selecting items from Appendices I and V, and then include a number of open-ended items. Think about making a self-evaluation of your teaching of the course and of how you might use discussions with students either before or after drawing up the questionnaire.

If you teach the course with other people you might wish to discuss with them the fact that you are thinking about evaluating your own contribution to the course and suggest that this offers a good opportunity to collect information on the course as a whole. Do not underestimate the threat that such a seemingly innocent and beneficial suggestion may pose to some of your colleagues. Approach this subject in a non-threatening way, involve and invite all concerned to contribute to the drawing up of the questionnaire. Also, reach clear agreement on who will receive what information. A course coordinator may take a leading role in all of this and in organizing subsequent sessions to consider the results, and where you go from here.

• *Where do I stand with regard to evaluating my lectures?*

The questions in Appendices I and V again provide a good starting point for evaluating your lectures. You can also ask for a colleague's comments by using the form given in Appendix IV. Think about self-evaluation and the use of discussions with students in drawing up or interpreting the questionnaire.

By all means ask a colleague if he or she would be interested in the two of you attending a few of each other's lectures in order to offer observation and comment. This is a better plan than simply asking a colleague to attend your lectures, as the latter can suggest an unequal power relationship and cast the visitor in the role of 'objective expert'. An experienced professor can learn something of value from a newly appointed lecturer, and under the collegial model, both are seen as colleagues trying to improve their performance by collaboration in a particular area of practice. Discuss the kinds of observation you should each make beforehand, perhaps basing these on the self-evaluation items outlined above. Bear in mind Scriven's (1988) comments concerning the status of visitors in the classroom, however, and use this process as a supplement to, rather than a replacement for, student evaluation of teaching.

• *Where do I stand with regard to evaluating my tutorials, seminars or practicals?*

Appendix V once more offers questions in each of these areas which may form a basis for drawing up a questionnaire. Do not be afraid to provide more open-ended questions for what may well be a smaller number of students involved. You might also find more of a place for discussion in the evaluation process with smaller groups, but bear in mind the warning given above on using unstructured discussion.

• *Where do I stand with regard to evaluating my supervision of research students?*

The supervision of research students has thus far been neglected. It is, of course, an important, though somewhat different, aspect of the lecturer's teaching role. The supervisory relationship is usually more intimate than the general relationship you have with students in large classes, and offers the opportunity of greater one-to-one contact. In your contacts with research students, bring up the subject of your own handling of the supervisory relationship. Are you being too dictatorial, or not offering enough advice . . . what are the main difficulties that students are facing at the moment . . . what can you do to help? You may want to ask students to complete an open-ended form towards the end of the supervisory process. On the form you can ask them to evaluate generally the supervision they have received, what was good about it and ways in which it could have been improved.

- *Should I start making systematic notes on my teaching?*

Following on from the short discussion of self-evaluation, you may want to think about allowing yourself time (for example at the end of the day or at home) to make some short notes about various aspects of your teaching during the day (or week) and the consequences of these for the next time you teach. Systematic consideration of these notes may be valuable in preparation for an institutional appraisal interview; the insights you have obtained and your subsequent plans for teaching in the future may provide an interesting area of discussion with your appraiser.

And finally

This has been a long chapter and a lot of ground has been covered. The main message has been that student evaluation of teaching is crucial in answering the question: 'Where am I now with my teaching?' If you cannot adequately answer this question, then do something about it now.

If you can share your intentions with colleagues in your department, with your appraiser, with colleagues from other departments or an educational development unit, then so much the better. Look for support wherever you can find it. Listen to what other people say about *their* teaching and the evidence they have for their opinions. Do not be afraid to share your own experiences. You are part of a culture which for too long has regarded the evaluation of teaching as 'too hard' a subject to tackle, a void, an unmentionable in polite conversation. This view is now being challenged and you need to decide what your own position will be, what difference you can make.

Notes

1. Three popular reviews of student evaluation of teaching are those by Cashin (1990), Marsh (1987) and Scriven (1988).
2. For many more ideas on evaluating your teaching (including checklists and forms) presented in interesting and accessible ways, see Gibbs *et al.* (1989) and O'Neil and Pennington (1992). See also Ramsden and Dodds (1989) for a good guide to the evaluation of courses and to the evaluation of teaching. Ramsden and Dodds draw a sharp distinction between *evaluation* (initiated and owned by teachers for developmental purposes only), *appraisal* (initiated by management for diagnostic and developmental purposes) and *performance assessment* (a tool of management focusing on competition, reward and punishment). While respecting this position, my own view is that it is often very difficult to distinguish purposes so

clearly. *Making the Most of Appraisal* is written to help lecturers reflect upon their careers and to spur them towards professional development, whether or not they take the insights thus gained into an appraisal interview. It is recognized, however, that the reality of the appraisal interview often finds lecturers wishing to raise interlinked issues involving evaluation, goal-setting, professional development, performance, resources, equity of treatment, advancement and promotion.

Chapter Five

Where am I going with my teaching?

Introduction

You may already have taken steps to evaluate your teaching, perhaps along the lines indicated in the previous chapter. The *ideal* order of events is probably something like this:

- evaluate your teaching;
- reflect on the evaluation evidence and try to understand and appreciate what it means;
- identify an area (of a course or of your teaching) which you are interested in developing;
- find out more about the area by talking to colleagues and educational development people, and by reading up on relevant educational development literature;
- make specific plans concerning your teaching, as suggested towards the end of this chapter;
- act, or carry out those plans;
- re-evaluate your teaching and start a new cycle of development.

This kind of process is along the lines of what is called an 'action research' cycle. Each cycle has the basic elements of: plan, act, observe, reflect. Having completed a cycle, you then move up to the next cycle, thus creating an upwardly moving spiral.

But things don't always work out so neatly in life. You may find yourself entering a cycle at almost any point. You may, for example, find yourself starting this chapter, and making plans for your teaching, without the benefits of student evaluations of your teaching. You may not have talked to anyone yet, nor looked at educational literature and resources. However, the very fact that you are thinking about looking at a particular issue which is of concern to you, or which you wish to develop, indicates that you have undergone *some* form of self-evaluation already. Equally, you probably have *some* idea about what it is that you want to try: what is likely to be your direction of change according to the new plan. So if you do not follow the ideal procedure outlined above, don't worry. It does not matter so much *where* you enter the process. It is of greater concern that you try to incorporate the elements of planning, acting, evaluating and reflecting irrespective of your entry point.

Teaching in the context of career

Let us start with the overall place you see teaching occupying in the future: where do you see teaching fitting in the context of your career as a whole? Do you, for example, see yourself primarily as a teacher who tries to do research when time permits? Do you see yourself as primarily a researcher, wishing to minimize time spent in all other areas? Do you think that your emphases have changed, or might change, during the course of your career? In order to help you put some of these things in perspective with regard to your own career, it might be helpful to consider some of the issues which have emerged from various studies concerned with the place of teaching in academic careers.

Most institutions give some guidance concerning the amount of time they consider their staff should spend in terms of teaching hours, and in terms of the percentage of time spent teaching as opposed to research and other responsibilities. In some institutions there is considerable flexibility, in others there are more rigidly applied conditions and criteria, and in all there are anomalies among subject areas and groupings of staff. If you are not already familiar with the policy your own institution operates regarding, for example, the number of hours you can be asked to teach, then you might wish to make enquiries. We all know, however, that a number put on maximum contact hours says little about the actual amount of time we can spend in preparation for, and development of, our teaching. That aside, it is still worthwhile to have an appreciation of the institutional position.

Some institutions have moved to a system where lecturers can nominate, usually within certain 'bands', the allocation of their time between the normal categories of teaching, research, administration, etc. This is an improvement on the fiction of academics being 'clones' who spend, for example, 50 per cent of their time teaching, 30 per cent doing research and 20 per cent administration. It is also in the best interests of the institution, for as Boyer (1990) comments:

> The quality of scholarship is dependent, above all else, on the vitality of each professor. Colleges and universities that flourish help faculty build on their strengths and sustain their own creative energies, throughout a lifetime (p. 43).
> [Note: Boyer is speaking from an American perspective where 'professor' and

'faculty' refer to most academic staff. Also, he uses 'scholarship' to incorporate all academic roles.]

There has always been considerable variation among staff as to how they allocate time between these and other areas, and in the way the pattern changes during a career. There is also the perennial problem of events conspiring to disrupt preconceived time allocation plans. This does not negate the idea of having an overall plan, however, as without it you may well become the victim of circumstance, rather than the architect of your own future. So what is a realistic plan for you in terms of your overall commitment in teaching? Some data from Halsey (1992, p. 186) are shown in Table 5.1.

Table 5.1 *Actual and ideal proportions of working time spent on teaching (%), 1989*

Type of Teaching	University		Polytechnic	
	Actual	*Ideal*	*Actual*	*Ideal*
Undergraduate	26	22	43	37
Graduate	12	15	7	11
Other	–	–	4	4

Halsey's survey was taken before the British polytechnics became universities, but it is probably still fair to say that the former polytechnics have maintained more of a teaching emphasis than other universities. The point could also be made with respect to the recent reorganization of Australian Higher Education. It is perfectly understandable, as a change of name does not make different histories disappear.

> The universities have better funding, more favourable staff-student ratios, and superior plant . . . . Polytechnic staff normally have a 17- to 19-hour-a-week teaching load in their contract (Halsey, 1992, p. 185).

If Halsey's survey is taken as a guide, it appears that somewhere between 38 per cent and 54 per cent of working time is spent on teaching, with these figures being close to the ideal viewed by academics (as we shall see later, this is not the case when it comes to research and administration).

Of course the amount of time spent teaching is not evenly distributed throughout the academic ranks. For example, Startup (1979), in a smaller (and older) survey found the distributions shown in Table 5.2.

Table 5.2 *Timetabled teaching hours per week (%)*

Hours	Professors	Readers and Senior Lecturers	Lecturers	All Staff
Fewer than 7	45.0	16.7	15.4	19.5
7–10	50.0	36.1	48.5	45.8
11–14	0.0	27.8	25.4	22.6
15 or more	0.0	16.7	7.7	8.9
Others (including don't knows)	5.0	2.8	3.1	3.2
Total	100.0	100.1	100.1	100.0
Number in sample	20	36	130	190*

*Includes four respondents who do not appear in earlier columns.
Source: Startup, 1979 p. 25.

This may give you some indication of relative weightings, and where you stand with regard to the amount of teaching you are called upon to do. How far these figures represent practices in your own institution or department is, of course, uncertain. While they give some idea about what can commonly occur, you really need to question for yourself how far your commitments are in line with those of your colleagues.

Many departments collect information from their staff about individual teaching commitments for the year, and use this to plan for an equitable share of workload. In some departments this is an open and participatory process, so that all can understand and appreciate what the actual position is, and why. In others, heads of departments regard such matters as their own exclusive domain, the resulting lack of information and rationale often leading to much rumour and speculation about who is and who is not 'pulling their weight' within the department. All we can do here is note that it is usually at the instigation of staff members, often due to frustration and dissatisfaction, that the allocation of teaching is opened up for discussion.

Teaching and research

For many of us, arriving at an arrangement whereby these two major aspects of our work are nicely balanced, and perhaps mutually supportive, is one of the hardest tasks we face. It is a task which is apparently impossible of completion. It seems that we have to renegotiate *constantly* and adjust the time we spend on teaching and the time we spend on research: year by year, day by day, even hour by hour. By planning and especially by monitoring how you spend your time, however, it should be possible to stay in touch with how your time allocation is going, what has intervened to disrupt your plans, what are the consequences and what adjustments can be made.

Making time for teaching

It may seem strange to talk about making time for teaching, as the experience of many academics is that it is far harder to make time for research (when we consider research we will look at that problem). However, there is still a question regarding the time you spend on teaching-related activities. In short, it is very easy for seemingly 'non-negotiable' aspects of teaching such as scheduled teaching periods and assignment marking to swallow up the whole of the time you allow for teaching. This can happen unless you make plans and set priorities concerning your teaching.

Making time for teaching means making time for important aspects of your role as a teacher which might otherwise be neglected. Certainly you need to make time available for such apparently 'non-negotiable' activities as preparation, class contact and marking. But these 'non-negotiables' are not necessarily evenly distributed throughout the year. It might be worthwhile considering each of these in turn to see when the peak times will occur in the year. You may be able to allocate time in your diary now and so plan for the more intense periods later. At the end of this section you will be invited to do this and to make plans for each semester, term, or even week.

But this is not the end of the story. You might also wish to reflect upon and evaluate your course while you are still teaching it (as outlined in the previous chapter) and to plan for the future both with regard to the development of your course and your own teaching-related knowledge and skill. Again, you might want to allocate time in your diary for these activities. For example, you may be able to allocate 15 minutes per week for reflecting on how your teaching has gone during the week and for evaluation. You might also plan for specific days to be identified and set aside at the end of the course (after the course evaluation and before exam marking) for thinking about the course and making plans for next year.

You may want to identify half an hour a week to be spent looking at teaching-related materials in the library. You might book into some of the sessions run by the staff or educational development unit at your institution. You could phone them up and see what they are likely to have on offer over the coming year. You might have suggestions of your own concerning areas in which you are interested. Alternatively, you could decide upon your own development agenda by setting aside in your diary some days to find out about topics which interest you (better lecturing, better tutorials, better assessment techniques, self-directed learning, etc). The point is that it is unlikely that changes will occur unless you actively plan for them.

Connecting teaching and research

One of the main things which it is claimed distinguishes 'higher' education is the close relationship which exists between teaching and research. The degree to which your teaching and research are related to each other can vary considerably. If you *can* improve the connection between your teaching and research, then this is surely for the better.

In an attempt to thwart the separation of funding for research and teaching, some senior university managers have talked about university teaching as 'research-based teaching'. Put crudely, it is claimed that higher education is concerned with teaching the knowledge which comes from research, that is, teaching *research knowledge*. At the same time, of course, we may well be teaching students how to conduct experiments or analyse texts, and thus be teaching *research skills*.

As you consider how you might better integrate your interests in teaching and research, you may well think of developing a new course in your particular research area. This is the time to give the matter serious consideration, perhaps to consult with your head of department and others, and to come up with a proposal. It is the most immediately obvious way of connecting your own teaching and research.

However, many of us have difficulty in drawing a straight line between our own research activities (knowledge or skills) and the courses or parts of courses which we teach. Some of us teach different courses in different areas from those we taught when we first started, while others of us have changed our research interests dramatically during our careers. For us, the simple formula of research-based teaching may be a fiction.

I do not think that is the end of the story, however. At a more general level, the fact that lecturers are actively engaged in research themselves provides the opportunity of interacting with students in a more collaborative and collegial way than that implied by a hierarchical teacher–student relationship. It opens the door for teachers to introduce talk of *processes* into their classes. For example, how do students go about writing essays or laboratory reports, making seminar presentations, working cooperatively with peers in a group project, seeking understanding of dense or difficult material or problem solving? Each of these has corollaries for lecturers in terms of *their own* writings for publication, lecturing or presenting conference papers, working cooperatively with colleagues in research (or teaching) projects, and their strategies for gaining understanding and problem solving. This might be called linking teaching and *research processes*.

The story does not end here either, as we can also turn the words around and instead of talking about teaching research, we can think about researching teaching. We may have been trained variously as biochemist, philosopher, surveyor, etc, and have maintained a research interest in the area. However, we are all teachers too, with a legitimate concern for our teaching, and for inquiring into and investigating how we can improve our professional practice or in other words, teach better.

Teachers in higher education *can* conduct research into their own teaching practices (or theories) and such research can be of considerable interest to their colleagues. It can lead to publication in subject journals (eg, *Journal of Subject X*), subject teaching journals (eg, *Journal of Subject X Education*,

Teaching Subject X) or one of the very many educational journals which might be relevant (eg, devoted to higher education, education generally, psychology and learning, teaching practices, educational technology, sociology and philosophy of education, educational research, educational administration, curriculum development, etc).

Here then are some areas concerning the relationship between teaching and research, which develop the relationship further than is often the case, and which you may care to think about in order to achieve a higher degree of integration between your own teaching and research. Some information on studies looking at the correlation between research productivity and evaluations of teaching is discussed in the next chapter: 'Where am I now with my research?'

New approaches to:

. . . teaching an old course

In considering where you are going in terms of developing your teaching, two alternative strategies might prove useful. You could take a look at one of your courses and consider ways of improving it; on the other hand, you could look at a particular teaching approach (lecturing or small group teaching, for example) and see how you could go about improving this, perhaps over a number of courses or year groups. Let us first consider new approaches to teaching an old course. (By 'old course' I don't necessarily mean that the course has been in existence and taught in the same way for 20 years, but that the course has been taught before by someone, not necessarily you.)

The first thing you need to decide is where your priorities lie in terms of developing the courses you teach. Suppose you teach part of the first-year course, and have courses of your own in the second and third year. It is very unlikely that you can systematically attempt a major evaluation of all of these at the same time. You need to establish priorities. So, out of the courses that you teach, which do you see as being in greatest need of rethinking? (As a hint, this will almost certainly be the course which is the hardest to tackle.) Does it make sense, for example, to concentrate on the first-year course this year, have a look at the third-year course next year and then the second-year course the following year?

How should you decide priorities? You will probably have an intuitive notion already about where to start, but some factors which you could bear in mind are:

- What things in your teaching cause you concern or worry you the most?
- Will any changes impact on a large or a small number of students?
- Will changes impact on 'non-committed' first-year students or 'committed' third-year students?
- Will changes impact on research/postgraduate students?

- What resources may be required, what are the likely costs in terms of staff time, tutors/demonstrators, equipment, etc?
- What resources are likely to be made available?
- What are departmental, faculty, and/or university priorities?
- What support are you likely to receive from the course leader, HOD, dean etc?
- What support are you likely to receive from colleagues?

With these kinds of criteria in mind, it should be possible to decide your priority for course improvement over the year ahead, and after that for your other courses over the following years.

If you have taken an evaluation of the course you wish to improve, or of your own teaching on the course, then you should already have some useful information to work from. If you have not, then perhaps your first step in improving the course should be to commit yourself to a thorough evaluation and review of the course this year. For information on how to do this, see the previous chapter of this book and Appendix items on the evaluation of teaching.

If you are looking for ideas on how to change your course, then it may pay to consult what has become a well established supply of resource materials on teaching and learning in higher education. There are now many books available and a considerable body of journal papers, so that it is likely you will find good resources on any aspect of teaching in which you might be interested. For a short, annotated bibliography of resources which you might consider in developing as a teacher, see Schwartz and Webb (1993, pp. 146–52).

There are also educational and staff development personnel whom you can contact at your own institution, or others. If you strike up a relationship with someone in educational development at your own institution, he or she should be able to point you towards resources and approaches which will be of value as you develop your course. This person may encourage you to take on the development of your course as an 'action research' project with a view to publication of the process and outcomes of your activities. You may decide to cooperate together on the project, and to involve others. You might also be pointed towards an educational development conference which you could attend, or a special interest or support group you could join. Once you have made the decision to start, the possibilities will begin to unfold.

. . . old teaching approaches

The other main way to go is to consider a teaching approach you have used in the past. Again, it is probably a good idea to decide on priorities first by considering some of the things you do routinely as a teacher (eg, the way you lecture, run small group tutorials, set and mark assignments, etc), and then make a decision as to which of these it is most important for you to scrutinize. Run through the list of factors outlined above in order to help make your decision.

If you have not done so already, you could evaluate one of your teaching approaches, perhaps doing so *across* courses. For example, if you are interested in lecturing, you could evaluate aspects of your lecturing to a number of different courses or classes. You could then look up materials on lecturing, and discuss the pros and cons of lecturing, lecturing skills, differing approaches which can be taken, and alternatives to lecturing, with someone from your educational development service. Once again, you might consider making your interest into the subject of an action research project, with a view to publication.

Perhaps we can now start to become a little more specific by looking at the ways in which some of the people we have already encountered in the case studies might approach the question of planning for the development of their teaching. This will serve as a useful halfway house before you make your own plans.

Where am I going with my teaching? The case studies

BARBARA (BRIAN) LANGTON

Summary reminder. *Barbara Langton is a relative newcomer to lecturing and will soon be facing a decision on tenure. She has had a very heavy teaching load, reorganizing and developing a number of courses. She has not published anything significant since joining the department, nor has she had the time to seek research funding.*

Teaching isn't my priority this coming year as I am trying to achieve a better balance between the amount of effort I put into teaching and research. All the same, I don't want to see all the hard work I have put into teaching over the past couple of years wasted. If all goes well I will be handing over some of my teaching to colleagues. I will go out of my way to help them with these courses and the changes, updating and improvements which have been made to them. I realize that this could be fraught with difficulty as people certainly don't want to be told how to do things and I will be opening myself up to the question: 'Why don't you continue doing it yourself?' I could also end up spending as much time helping out as teaching the things myself. But there must be a middle way, and that is what I will try to find. My objectives are clear, if difficult:

- Discuss the teaching I am handing over with those colleagues who are taking it up. Make available and discuss with them the course structure, the way the lectures, tutorials and labs have been run, the assessments, and give them all of the materials I have produced.
- Do this in a non-threatening, helpful ('ever-so humble') way – 'I wondered if these would be of use . . . they aren't perfect but you're very welcome to what I have . . . we found this way of doing it worked very well and the students said they found it really helpful . . .' – that sort of thing.

MICHAEL (MICHELLE) RICHARDS

Summary reminder. *Michael Richards is also a relatively new lecturer coming up for tenure. He has previous commercial and industrial experience but is enjoying the flexibility of an academic position. He has not had much to do with other people in the department. Michael has nearly completed a PhD; he published a couple of papers last year and has considerable PhD research material remaining. He has recently had a poor student evaluation of his teaching.*

In thinking about my teaching for next year, I am concerned about the poor teaching evaluation I received for my part of the large first-year lecture course last year. I have now talked to a few people who know about the evaluation of teaching, and read some of the material on it, and I'm a bit more convinced than I was about the validity of what I used to call the 'popularity contest'. Anyway, I don't think that I can simply ignore the results of the survey; I want to do something to improve matters.

Having worked through the results of the standard evaluation form I can easily see where the problem lies. It seems to be firmly in the area of stimulating the students' interest in the subject. They also don't see me as being very helpful, which is a bit of a surprise.

I wonder how much I am paying the price for teaching on this course with a couple of 'showmen', or should I say 'show persons', as one is a woman. Because I was new to teaching the course, I attended a few of their lectures and I have to say they were very impressive. They are both experienced teachers, have been teaching the course for a good few years, and are very lively and enthusiastic. It's not just show, of course, they know what they are talking about too. They have both worked out in commerce and have lots of examples and anecdotes to illustrate the things they are talking about in their lectures. I enjoyed their lectures a lot, but never really thought about changing my own stuff. To be honest, I have been glad just to get the lectures, all the OHPs and the like, ready for the next session. I haven't had time to think about 'entertaining' as well.

I may not be a born entertainer but I am willing to think about changing what I do in order to try to stimulate more interest. I *am* interested and enthusiastic about the subject, myself, although this is obviously not coming across. I need to find out more about this whole area.

I will also start to look at postgraduate supervision. I am now thinking quite seriously about starting a funded research project which would employ a couple of postgraduate students. I saw this as being a few years away, but I recently met up with a former colleague from the commercial world and we both thought that now was a good time to make a proposal, as there is funding money around. Everything could happen much faster than I had been thinking. But I haven't got a clue where to start with regards to supervision. My supervisor was ok, but I would like to think that I could do better. I will find out about this area too. So, to answer the question of where am I going with my teaching next year, I guess I would say something like this:

- I intend to improve the student evaluations of my teaching.
- To do this I will find out about how I can create more student interest in my classes.
  I will also try to make my part of the course more relevant to the students and

think about doing this through examples, and perhaps get them to work through case examples. I will try this and see how it works. I will look for some advice from my colleagues who share the teaching of the first-year course, and from someone in the educational development unit.

- I will find out more about why the students don't see me as being very helpful, and do something about it.
- I will see if there is any information about on postgraduate supervision – in order to prepare myself for this.

JANET (JOHN) SMITH

Summary reminder. Janet Smith has tenure and has published very successfully. She has had good student evaluations of her lectures, less so of her tutorials. She is very forceful in committee work. Janet is ambitious to advance and is frustrated that she is not advancing quickly enough. She is beginning to think about moving elsewhere.

I am quite satisfied with the way that my lecture courses are going and the teaching evaluations of these have been good. My tutorials haven't been evaluated so highly, however, especially, and surprisingly, my honours group tutorials. I really want students to talk and argue in my tutorials but they simply won't. They never prepare very well either, and so I have to step in to fill in the things they don't know. I always end up lecturing. The first-year students seem to like this, but the honours group appears to be a bit more hostile.

I know that I come over as a bit daunting, a bit aggressive, and that I tend to dominate. That seems to work well in lectures. But I would quite like to be able to make people feel a bit more at ease in my company, to bring them out rather than bowl them over with my brilliance (joke). I recognize this when I see it being done well and I am very envious of the ability some people seem to have here. My mentor could do it (she always encouraged me to work things out for myself) and so too can my present HOD (he is wonderful in difficult departmental meetings). I have just taken over coordination of the first-year course, which will mean that I have to work with a lot of other people, such as colleagues who share the lecturing, student tutors and the student representatives. That could be interesting. So where am I going? . . . somewhere like this:

- I will take steps to improve student evaluations of my tutorials.
- I will find out if there are any techniques I can use to make students take a larger part in my tutorials.
- I will see if I can teach myself some new tricks about relating to my tutorial groups. I will put in for my 'Facilitator Grade A' certificate (joke).
- I will try and find out more about the skills I think I need (and don't have) which will enable me to adopt a different approach not only to my tutorial groups, but also in other meeting and group situations. I want to have a choice in how I behave, because I don't at the moment and I think the manner I adopt is sometimes counter-productive. Perhaps I could try some of this stuff out in coordinating the first-year course.

Paul (Pauline) Whiting

Summary reminder. Paul Whiting has been a lecturer for many years and has been at the career grade for a considerable time but has never applied for promotion beyond it. He has a grown-up family and no thoughts of leaving the university. He has not published anything recently despite having plenty of ideas. He is very committed to and enthusiastic about teaching although he has never taken a student evaluation of his teaching. The HOD has raised the possibility that he might take over some of the appraisal interviews in the department next year.

I've never done one of the teaching evaluation things. I think I'm a good teacher anyway. But there does seem to be more pressure coming on us to do evaluations these days, and I reckon that I will get into it next year. From what I gather I can do a *feedback* type of evaluation anytime to see how things are going. I reckon that I will do that for each of the main courses I teach about halfway through term one. At the end of my teaching I will do the formal evaluation. I am also interested in the idea of a teaching portfolio. Seeing that I have put such a lot of my time into teaching, it would be nice to be able to document this in some way, especially if my career starts to move forward again.

I am still interested in using computers in my teaching. I want to find out more about doing this, and perhaps start up a project to see how it goes. If I get a paper out of it, so much the better. I think the education development people have helped run projects like this before and so I could start there. Anywhere would be a help, as I haven't a clue about how you would set up a project like this and write it up. Do you need a control group *not* using computers, and lots of statistics? I haven't a clue about that, but my overall intentions for the coming year are fairly clear:

- I will run feedback evaluations of the courses I teach and use this information to see if I can improve my teaching. I will also run standard end-of-year evaluations, and find out how to construct a teaching portfolio.
- I will find out how I should go about setting up a project on using computers in one of my courses. I intend to introduce computers, and might as well do it in such a way that it can be evaluated and written up as a piece of research.

Charles (Carol) Ross

Summary reminder. Charles Ross is professor and head of department. He is heavily involved in both departmental and university-level administration. Charles retains a fairly full teaching load, but has not published much over the last ten years. He has also lost contact with the international research organization on which he once served. He is contemplating the prospect of retirement in a few years' time.

Teaching isn't really an issue for me this year. I will run my courses pretty much along the lines they were run last year – it's a bit late to start teaching an old dog new tricks. The one thing I could perhaps do, however, is keep a better grip on the tutorial side, and what the tutors are getting up to. I have an outline of what should be covered, week by week, but I must admit it is pretty skimpy. What I might do is put some more flesh on the bones so that the tutors have more guidance as to what I am expecting.

Last year it seems the tutorials were a bit variable, and depended on how good the particular tutor was. I suppose I could also arrange some training for the tutors and keep in better contact with them. It seems as if I have some objectives after all:

- Issue new and expanded guidelines for tutors taking the tutorials associated with my lecture course. Give a better indication of what is to be covered and how.
- Arrange for tutors to attend a training session in the first week of term. The educational development people should be able to put this on. I will attend it myself to see if it is any good.
- Arrange regular meetings for tutors to report on problems, improvements, etc. I can discuss with them how often these will be held.

Your turn

It is now your turn to think about and make some plans regarding your teaching. As before, it is a good idea for you to make notes as you consider the questions which follow. It would also be a good idea for you to have your diary and year planner (or computer calendar and planner) available while you work through the questions. In order to provide some structure in considering the questions which follow, they are grouped into similar areas to those which have been used previously in this chapter.

- *How do I see teaching in terms of my career overall?*

How important is teaching in the overall context of your career at the moment? Has it become more or less important than it was? Why? What role do you think teaching will play as your career develops in the future?

If you were to choose how you would allocate percentages of your time with regard to teaching, research, administration, etc, how would you do this; what would the figures be? What does this tell you about the place you see teaching occupying in your career at the moment, and about the way you *actually* allocate your time?

How does your teaching workload compare with others in your department? If you do not know, could you find out? How would you go about this?

- *How can I make time for teaching?*

What actual amount of time do you see yourself allocating for preparation, teaching and marking? Have you allowed for these by allocating time in your diary and year planner and by making semester, term or weekly plans?

How will you allocate time for reflecting upon and evaluating your course while you are still teaching it, for planning for the future with regard to your teaching and for the development of both your course and your own teaching-related knowledge and skill? Can you plan and set aside time for these activities now by allocating time in your diary?

- *How will I evaluate the courses I teach?*

List each aspect of your teaching duties starting with the courses or parts of courses which you teach. Identify those for which you have recently obtained student and peer evaluations. For the rest, make a commitment and plan for evaluation over the next three years. You will need to decide when and how the evaluations will be made, and what kind of evaluation (feedback, institutional, mixed) is needed.

- *How will I evaluate my various teaching approaches?*

Having identified the courses or parts of courses which you teach, think now about the different ways in which you teach. For example, indicate which of the following (or other) approaches you use: lecturing, tutorials, seminars, laboratories, field work, clinical, distance, computer-based, case-based, problem-based, self-directed. Again, which of these have you already evaluated, and can you make a plan to consider over the next three years the approaches which you have not previously evaluated?

- *Can my interest areas in teaching and research be better integrated?*

Do you want to propose and teach a course which is nearer to your research interests? Write a brief justification for the new course, and what you envisage as its impact on other courses (would you drop a present course; does the new course support or complement others?). Outline what the course would look like, the level and kinds of students who would be likely to take it and the people who would teach it. Outline a process which would be likely to see it being accepted (eg, whose backing is it important to gain; should you raise the proposal informally to start with; when and where should the formal proposal be made, etc?).

Can you see any merit in developing your teaching by introducing research and teaching processes used by both yourself *and* your students (eg, developing writing, oral presentations, working cooperatively, problem solving)? How could you do it? (You may need to consult resource people and materials before attempting this.)

What area of your own teaching would you like to know more about and to research? Are you interested in the prospect of such research leading to publication? Would you see this as representing an opportunity for collaborative research with a colleague? Are there any funds available (such as teaching development grants) for which you could apply? Can you talk to someone about conducting educational or action research (eg, members of an educational development unit)?

- *What course development work should I undertake?*

Look at the list of your major teaching commitments again and rank them in terms of their need for development (you may wish to look at the factors which appeared earlier in this chapter). Sketch out a three-year plan for developing the courses in which you are involved. Make a more detailed development plan for next year concerning the course you have chosen as being most in need of attention.

- *Do I want to examine a particular teaching approach?*

Make a list of the main approaches to teaching which you use (eg, lecturing, small group discussions, setting essays or multiple choice test items, etc). Decide which one of these is most in need of attention and development. Devise a plan of how you will improve upon this teaching approach (again, you may need to consult resource people and materials).

Consider choosing one teaching approach with which you are *unfamiliar* (eg, problem-based learning, case-based learning, self-directed learning, self- or peer assessment, using computers in teaching, etc). Consult people who should know about this approach and ask them for references so that you can read up on it. Make a list of pros and cons which would be associated with using the approach in some form or other in your teaching. Decide whether the new approach you have read about has any scope for use in your own teaching.

- *What is my action plan for teaching or course development?*

Having worked through the questions above, you now need to draw together your thoughts and the insights you have gained, to allocate priorities, and to decide on an action plan. It will help to make the objectives you set yourself as clear as possible, and to have a good idea of how you can assess if the objective has been met successfully. For example, Michael (Michelle) Richards set himself the objectives of making his lectures both more interesting and more relevant to his students. To test this objective, and as part of his overall teaching evaluation, he could ask questions concerning how interesting and how relevant students found his part of the course. He could also ask for open-ended comment on which particular parts of the course they found interesting (and why) and which parts they did not. This information could help him make 'second round' changes.

Other things you should bear in mind in writing your action plan are that you do not set yourself too many objectives, that they are realistic and attainable (but still challenging), and that you specify a timetable of events. This last point means that you plan exactly when you will begin, how long you will proceed before taking stock of what is happening (monitoring and evaluating), and when you intend to end.

In Janet (John) Smith's case, for example, she might decide to ask someone from the educational development unit to process open-ended responses from her tutorial groups toward the end of the second semester, to consider the responses and to do some reading on tutorial teaching over the holidays. She will then plan a new strategy for the beginning of next year, run an evaluation of how things are going mid-way through the semester and a final one at the end of the course. At the same time she will shadow this by asking for comments from her colleagues concerning her performance on the committee which she chairs, this process following a similar time-scale to the tutorial project.

You should also consider who can help you, or to whom you can talk about your plans. Being able to talk over your ideas and plans with a trusted colleague can offer the opportunity for reinforcement and encouragement, together with a different viewpoint which may provide valuable suggestions. For example, it may have been one of Janet's colleagues who pointed out to her that some of her tutorial groups are quite small, and that students may be unwilling to be critical if they are unsure about anonymity. This colleague may have suggested to Janet that she let the educational development unit process the responses – retype and categorize them – and that she could work with one of the unit's staff members on improving her tutorials.

- *How will you approach the question of 'where you are going with your teaching' in the appraisal interview?*

Can you bring the insights you may have developed in working through this chapter into your next appraisal interview? Do you want to discuss your long-term objectives with regard to the place of teaching in your career? What aspects of your objectives and plans for next year's teaching do you want to discuss in the appraisal interview? Do the short-term teaching plans which you already have, or which you are developing, make sense in terms of your longer-term objectives? What do you think will be the stance taken by your appraiser concerning your teaching for next year?

Summary

In drawing up an action plan concerning where you are going with your teaching, you might consider the following points:

- Long-term objectives for your teaching.
- Short-term objectives (ie, next year) for your teaching.
- How will the objectives be met; what is your plan?
- Time-frame for achieving your objectives (start, monitoring, end).
- Who can help or assist you; to whom can you talk?
- How will you monitor the process, see if you are making progress?
- How will you evaluate how successful you have been in meeting your objectives; how do you know?
- What do you want to raise and discuss in the appraisal interview; what do you want to avoid?

Chapter Six

Where am I now with my research?

Introduction

In this chapter we will consider the place of research in the context of your career. Most academics know the importance of research and publication for increasing their prospects of promotion. Publish or perish, with few exceptions, is as prevalent today as it ever was. In fact the pressure to publish has lately been extended. Many lecturers in the former UK polytechnics and in the newly amalgamated universities of Australia have recently been subjected to this pressure. 'New' universities have developed plans and appointed staff to assist in the development of a 'research culture', and thus to ensure their institutions do not miss out on research funding.[1] So, whether you have always worked in a context where research is viewed as important, or whether you are facing this challenge for the first time, it is possible that you feel yourself to be under pressure with regard to research and publication. You are not alone in this. Richard Startup (1985) took surveys in a provincial British university in the 1970s and 80s, with the results shown in Table 6.1.

Not surprisingly, Startup's figures show that junior staff felt themselves to be under more pressure to publish, although it is interesting that many senior academics still feel the pressure too (mainly in order to maintain their reputation and as an example to junior colleagues, according to Startup). But why do academics feel this pressure; why is publication of such importance?

Table 6.1 *Felt pressure to publish (percentages)*

| | 1982–3 | | | | 1972–3 |
	Professors	Readers and Senior Lecturers	Lecturers	All Respondents	All Respondents
Great pressure	11.8	14.5	30.7	24.2	25.8
Some pressure	82.4	69.1	61.4	65.6	60.5
No pressure	5.9	12.7	7.9	9.1	13.2
Others (eg, don't knows)	0.0	3.6	0.0	1.1	0.5
	100.1	99.9	100.0	100.0	100.0
N	17	55	114	186	190

Source: Startup, 1985, p. 72.

Why publish?

The findings from Startup's surveys confirm what we already know, and are summed up in the words of one of his respondents: 'Pressure derives from the failure of the university to accept any other criteria for promotion' (p. 72). In the language of psychology, such a reason would be termed 'extrinsic': the driving force being that of 'external motivation' for rewards which reside beyond the control of the individual. In terms of *pressure to publish*, this was by far the most cited reason given by Startup's respondents.

The other main reason could be termed 'intrinsic', or driven by 'internal motivation'. Indeed, the earlier survey conducted by Startup (1979), showed that the major reason given by respondents *for doing research* was 'because one enjoys doing it', with 92 per cent responding in this way. The personal fulfilment which we as academics experience from taking on a particular research project and seeing it through to publication, is obviously of immense satisfaction to us. It takes us close to the values of academic freedom and autonomous inquiry which are supposed to lie at the heart of higher education. The personal enjoyment of 'getting it right' or 'doing it well' are as real to the university academic as they are to the school child.

Other reasons given by academics for doing research and for feeling the pressure to publish are for personal prestige, to attract funding, for financial reward, because they consider it their duty, and to enliven their teaching. Again, it is possible to identify aspects of internal and external motivation associated with these reasons, but it is not necessary to get too carried away with thinking about motivation to do research in terms of this polarity. From my own experience, and from talking to colleagues, our reasons for doing research and for publishing are often complex, intertwined, paradoxical and changeable.

For example, promotion may mean more money, but it also means greater prestige and academic status. If it were possible to separate these out, my guess is that many of us are at least as interested in academic rank, reputation and our status within the profession or the university, as we are in money. And if academic rank and reputation is an important aspect of how others see us, can we divorce this from how we see ourselves? In other words, by doing research and by publishing, we may not only be trying to justify ourselves to others, but perhaps also to still the self-doubts we retain about our own abilities. We may be attempting to bolster and secure our professional self-esteem and self-regard. This is the kind of thing I mean by suggesting that there are complex reasons which sustain us in what, for many of us, is a difficult and isolated part of our lives as academics.

Of course we may be concerned when a 'rival' is promoted ahead of us, but it is interesting to question whether or not this is sufficient to sustain us in research. Becher (1989) quotes the mathematician G H Hardie as saying that the 'dominant incentives to research' are 'intellectual curiosity, professional pride, and ambition', which together constitute 'desire for reputation' (p. 53). An overly mechanistic view of the main motive force behind research being simply for promotion misses the importance of the combination of these factors. It is this blend of curiosity, creativity, ambition, pride, the need for recognition and for self-esteem, which together make the challenges and opportunities associated with research so important to us, and accounts for the subtlety of the relationship we have with our research.

Research and teaching

Are those who have substantial publications records, on average, better or worse at teaching than those who have not? This question in different guises comes up in many places, from staff coffee lounges to departmental meetings considering the allocation of teaching. The arguments often run something like this:

- Good researchers make good teachers because they pass on their enthusiasm for the subject. Active researchers are constantly refreshed by their creative research activity, they are up to date; they stimulate students and motivate them towards research. Researchers serve as models in terms of the hard work, discipline and dedication necessary for research, and this transfers into their classroom activities.
- Good researchers make lousy teachers because the only way to find the large amount of time and commitment necessary for research is at the expense of teaching. Prodigious producers of research exploit their colleagues and their students for their own career advancement. They do not put time into the running of the department, nor time into students, other than their own research students. They put as little time, thought and effort into teaching as possible. Their research areas are usually so far removed from or such a small part of the main undergraduate programme that they *should not* have much of an impact on students anyway.

According to the (somewhat limited) research evidence on the relationship between research productivity and teaching performance, neither of these positions appears to be the case. To my knowledge, the most comprehensive work in this area is Feldman's (1987) review of over 40 American studies. He found that overall, there was only a very small positive relationship ($r=0.12$) between research productivity and teaching effectiveness (from the 29 studies which allowed statistical aggregation). So, while it appears that being a productive researcher (usually in terms of the number of papers published) is not associated with terrible teaching (usually in terms of student evaluations), neither is there strong evidence for research productivity being associated with superior teaching. Further investigation of the data also allowed Feldman to suggest the following.

> High producers of research, compared with low producers, are no less likely (nor any more likely) to be friendly in class, to show concern for students, to encourage discussions, to be open to others' opinions, or to be sensitive to class level and progress. Nor are they more likely – indeed, they may be a little less likely – to be intellectually narrow and to assign course material that is either overly specialised or overly sophisticated for students (p. 278).

> There is almost no support . . . for the proposition that time or effort devoted to research is inversely related to teaching effectiveness either in some direct way or indirectly through its negative effects on teacher's preparation and organisation, quality of the teacher's feedback to students, or the teacher's helpfulness and availability (p. 264).

> . . . increments of time spent on research . . . were associated with only small decrements on time or effort devoted to teaching . . . and more from decrements in time spent in leisure activities and with family or friends (p. 267).

So while the evidence is somewhat limited, it appears that a case for research productivity and teaching quality being strongly associated in *either* a positive *or* a negative way still needs to be made: the evidence to date is that there is no strong association.

Research and scholarship

At this point I think it necessary to say a few words about research and the associated notion of scholarship. My own position on this is that the better the job we make of our research, the better scholarship we display. As John Kingman (1993) has argued, 'scholarly' is a quality, or a description, which may or may not accompany our research and publication activities, or indeed, our teaching. There have been recurrent attempts to redefine and debase scholarship into a kind of teaching-related research ('keeping up to date', etc.), and to separate this from 'real' research. Such moves commonly make mistakes by suggesting that knowledge is either new or recycled, either basic or applied, that basic research has to be expensive, and that empiricism is the model for all other kinds of research. They also usually accompany attempts to reduce research funding. But scholarship is a quality, not an activity. One cannot spend the evening 'doing scholarship', as one can doing research. For this reason, and so as to avoid confusion, I have tried not to use the term 'scholarship' in this book. Instead I use 'research' to cover the 'research' activities of all academics, be they in the arts, humanities, sciences, social sciences, commerce, the professions, or whatever.[2]

Evaluating research

In order to be evaluated, research has to be accessible for comment, discussion, debate and challenge. For this to be possible usually means that research has to be published. The main way for a person's research to be evaluated is therefore to evaluate that person's publications. It is one of the curious commonplaces of universities that it is possible to evaluate publications objectively, but that it is not possible to do the same for teaching. In fact, of course, evaluation of *both* is possible. Each may be evaluated crudely and mechanistically or more sensitively and appropriately. Both call for varying sources of data and for subjective judgement. The art and craft of evaluation is at the same time as difficult and as necessary with regard to research, as it is to teaching. We must all hope and trust that this art, closely akin to what Elliot Eisner (1985) calls 'connoisseurship', is alive and well in our institutions.

What sources of evidence are used in evaluating publication? The ones I will consider are: peer review, citation counts, number of publications and number and value of research grants and contracts. In doing so I will be quite selective and will not consider, for example, research assessment exercises which seek to rank institutions or departments, nor the processes of funding councils. That having been said, some of the points made below generalize to other areas.

Peer review

Journal editors and reviewers

Before an article is published there is usually a refereeing process, in which a number of people (often three) who are regarded as being qualified to do so, make comments on the quality and suitability for publication of the manuscript submitted. Papers are thus evaluated as a precursor to their publication, and if this evaluation process was uniform, then the number of papers which a person has published could be defended as a reasonable indicator of that person's research productivity. I suppose this is what lies behind the way we list our publications under headings such as 'papers in *refereed international* journals'. It sounds good, and suggests uniformity. Note, however, that even with a uniform system of evaluation, the *number* of publications a person has would give no indication as to their *quality*.

Of course the evaluation process for submitted papers is very far from being uniform. Some journals (including respected professional journals) do not have an independent refereeing procedure at all, and there is enormous variation among subject areas, readership, number of potential contributors and the publishing objectives of journals. Some journals have a readership and potential contributors numbering in the tens of thousands, while others are lucky to reach a few hundred. Some journals reject well over 90 per cent of the manuscripts they receive, while others have to persuade people to make contributions, and subsequently publish nearly everything they receive. Again, this does not necessarily say anything about the quality of papers which are published. Some of the currently most prestigious journals had lowly origins, and some of the most innovative work has appeared in obscure places. This can happen when well established and conservative journal editors and referees use their role as gatekeepers to keep out what they see as fringe, radical, misguided or wrong. They become protectors of the orthodox and mainstream, enemies of the new.

The label 'international' brings its own problems too. It is certainly no assurance of high quality, just as a journal being local or national does not necessarily indicate inferiority. In some areas, for example, knowledge tends to be quite locally specific and so the comparative or international dimension may be somewhat underdeveloped in comparison with the volume of local writing. Law is sometimes cited as being in this category, where the difference between the legal codes of countries tends to encourage local publication. Non-international journals, in this case, may be among the most prestigious.

So how reliable is the process of peer review when an article has been submitted to a journal for publication? In a word, it appears to be *variable*. For example, Morrow *et al.* (1992) quote the correlations shown in Table 6.2 between (on average two) reviewers for a number of journals.

Table 6.2 *Interrater reliability from various journals*

Journal	Reliability (R)
American Psychologist	.70
Developmental Review	.61
Journal of Educational Psychology	.51
Physiological Zoology	.47
Journal of Experimental Education	.46
New England Journal of Medicine	.46
Social Problems	.45
Journal of Personality and Social Psychology	.41
Research Quarterly for Exercise and Sport	.37
Personality and Social Psychology Bulletin	.35
Journal of Abnormal Psychology	.32
Medical Journals*	.17–.40

* Various unnamed medical journals cited in Ciccheti and Conn (1978).

In another study of well known psychology journals, Peters and Ceci (1982) selected 12 papers written by respected authors from top university departments in North America. They then resubmitted these papers as new manuscripts to the journals which had published them some 18–32 months before. The only changes they made to the originals concerned the name and affiliation of authors, together with some very minor amendment to the title, abstract and first paragraph. Nine of the twelve re-submissions went unnoticed, and eight of these were rejected by the editors and referees.

The implication is that name, status and affiliation carry some weight when it comes to the publication of articles. And while editors always know the names and affiliations of those submitting papers, referees can often work this out too, even when they are sent a manuscript 'blind'. Ceci and Peters (1984) found, for example, that over a third of referees could still work out who the author was, even though they had been sent the manuscript 'blind'. There is some evidence that book reviewers are more favourably disposed towards authors of the same sex, and that such things as political allegiance, in certain contexts, can have an effect too (Abramowitz *et al.*, 1975; Moore, 1978).

Book publishing

A proposal for a new book also goes through a peer and publisher review process where most of the arguments outlined with respect to journal articles also apply. However, the bottom line in determining whether a book is published or not is somewhat different. Journals already have a 'captured' market, whereas each book has to capture its own. In other words, the bottom line in determining whether a book will be published is: will it sell, is it economically viable? The academic, scientific and, let us use the word, scholarly, worth of the book may be beyond reproach. The referees' comments may be glowing, the credentials of the author formidable and the topic of the book important. But academic values are not the crucial determinant of whether a book is published or not. Sales are.

This is of course simplifying matters somewhat, as a book proposal which receives strong academic backing may convince a publisher that it will do well in the market place. But it is a case of addition (strong academically *plus* saleable) rather than synonymity (strong academically *equals* saleable). In terms of the evaluation of our own research and publications, this brings into question any notion that a simple equation may be made between book publication and academic worth.

Head of department, referees

Many institutions call upon the head of department, dean or similar person to rate research and publications performance as part of the promotions procedure. This rating or report is often taken very seriously by promotions committees as they weigh the relative merits of candidates. That this is so makes it all the more imperative that the person who is writing about a person's research and publication record does so from a position of intimate acquaintance and balanced judgement. This is not always the case.

When peer assessment is important, the crucial question is usually, 'Who are the peers?' Where there is only one (ie, head of department), and if his or her assessment is not openly available to be challenged, then there is the possibility for suspicion and distrust to develop. The risk is reduced if more than one person is asked to comment, and if the person making the promotion application (or filling in an appraisal form) is able to nominate referees of his or her own.

Citation counts

Yes it does, and increasingly so. Seen as an 'objective' and 'value-free' way of avoiding the subjective judgements of peer review, the argument is that by counting the number of times an author's work is cited by others, a precise and objective way has been found of assessing the impact of an author's work. Simple, objective, numerical and cheap: one can see why citation counting has increased in popularity. Add to this 'universality', with the Institute for Science Information (ISI) in Philadelphia supplying all of the most frequently used sources: the *Science Citation Index*, the *Social Science Citation Index* and the *Arts and Humanities Citation Index*. The realization of one standard and universally accepted source is every evaluator's dream. And the ready availability of citation indices has led to the growth of citation analysis as a research industry in its own right. A number of disciplines, for example, have citation research workers who report on such things as the 'top 50' workers in the field.

But citation counting has its problems and critics too. The best critique of citation counting I have seen is by Chapman (1989). It is an interesting article as it applies to citation counting in psychology, and psychology has concerns in the natural and social sciences, and the humanities. Many of the points which Chapman makes are thus relevant over a range of disciplines. And Chapman identifies 25 or more shortcomings associated with ISI citation counts, some of which are as follows:

- Some journals are not considered, especially non-English language ones.
- Books are excluded, which means the exclusion of much theoretical and integrative literature.
- Much (important) applied research is excluded as this appears in reports and working papers, etc.
- Referencing conventions pose problems, especially with regard to the citing of editors. There is little consistency with regard to the citing of editors of journals, books, monographs, series, etc.
- Letters, abstracts and book reviews can be used. One way to boost one's citation count according to Garfield (1974) is thus to publish 'a controversial letter on a subject of wide interest in a leading journal. The letter should contain several gross errors in order to elicit the maximum number of subsequent correction letters with appropriate citations'.
- One citation is one citation (irrespective of the quality or rejection rate of the journal). Also, one citation only is recorded, irrespective of how many or how few times the source is cited in a particular paper.

- First authors *only* gain credit because articles and not authors are recorded. Second or subsequent authors can look up first-author citations on their papers, but people other than authors are unlikely to do this.
- 'Stars' dominate. Citations are even more strongly associated with a small group of authors than are simple number of publication counts.
- Authors with the same surnames and initials can be scrambled, married women who have changed their names can lose out, and a person may find him or herself in several locations because of inconsistencies in abbreviating first names and initials.
- Newcomers miss out as it takes time for citations to work their way into the literature.
- Citation does not imply approval as papers may be cited because they are poor, defective or fraudulent.

Apart from these points we must return to the fact that citation does not indicate quality. The shortest of abstracts from a conference proceeding will count equally with a voluminous and trend-setting paper in the best of journals.

Nor does citation necessarily indicate impact on a particular discipline. An interesting example is given by Endler *et al.* (1978) who asked the most cited psychologists what works had the most impact on them. Kurt Lewin came up as the second most important influence on these eminent psychologists, but he was only the 49th most cited author, and in an earlier citation listing he did not feature at all. A number of other examples of this effect have also been reported.

Finally, there are markedly different expectations across disciplines, which makes cross-discipline comparisons very difficult. A paper in a well developed area of philosophy may take years to produce and this could also be the case for an ethnographic study involving several years of fieldwork. On the other hand, the result of an empirical laboratory study may be published a matter of months after the experiment was conducted. A scientific paper reporting the result of an investigation might be only a few pages long, and may have a number of co-authors. On the other hand, a historian might work on a single-authored book for many years. Some disciplines tend to cite a great deal, some comparatively little; some tend to cite and include new work quickly, some do not. There are thus many dangers, pitfalls, and shortcomings associated with citation counting: it is far from being a simple and objective mechanism to rescue us from the subjectivity of evaluation.

Number of publications

Many of the points which have just been made about the pitfalls of citation counting also apply to publication counting. Publication counting says nothing about quality, and is prone to the same cross-discipline differences which affect citation counting. However, it is still probably the most widespread indicator of research productivity and, in its favour, it does not exhibit the 'stars' phenomenon to such a marked degree as citation counting. In other words, although a small number of authors account for a very large number of papers published, this applies even more so to citation counts.

While we might know all of the reasons why the number of publications on our cv does not give a very good indication as to the scope and quality of our research, it still seems to remain of considerable interest to us. Many of us would be too embarrassed to ask a new colleague how many publications he or she has. But many of us find it enthralling to view the cvs of job applicants, colleagues, acquaintances, visitors to the department, etc, when such opportunities arise. The question we are obviously asking ourselves as we do this is: 'How am I doing in comparison with others?'

There is no easy answer to this question. That is why promotions committees agonize on these matters for so long and still manage to displease so many. Aggregate information should be treated with enormous care, but aggregate data there are, and they make interesting reading.

Startup's (1985) surveys in the early 1970s and 80s showed that in terms of all of his respondents (about 190 each time), quite a change occurred during the period (see Table 6.3). In 1972–3, nearly 40 per cent had five publications or fewer and about 25 per cent had more than 20 publications. By 1982–3 the percentage with five publications or fewer had almost halved, while the percentage with more than 20 publications had almost doubled. And nowhere is the competition tougher than in the pure sciences, where according to Startup's information, over 60 per cent of his respondents had more than 20 publications.

Table 6.3 *Number of publications (percentages)*

| Number of publications | 1982–3 | | | | | 1972–3 |
	Arts	Social Studies	Pure Sciences	Applied Sciences	All Respondents	All Respondents
0–5	41.3	38.5	7.5	12.8	21.5	38.9
6–11	19.6	26.9	11.9	25.6	18.3	18.9
12–20	8.7	7.7	17.9	10.3	12.9	15.3
Over 20	28.3	26.9	62.7	48.7	46.2	23.7
Others (eg, don't knows)	2.2	0.0	0.0	2.6	1.1	3.2
	100.1	100.0	100.0	100.0	100.0	100.0
N	46	26	67	39	186*	190

*Includes eight respondents who do not appear in earlier columns. Source: Startup, 1985, p. 76.

It should be remembered that we are talking about simple counts of publications here which take no account, for example, of the length of the paper. In a now dated study, Rudd and Hatch (1968) weighted publications from half a unit (for a jointly-authored paper) to five units for a single-authored book. Using such measures they produced the following index of publications for various subject areas (number of respondents given in brackets):

Technology	3.35	(151)
Science	5.17	(680)
Social studies	8.59	(55)
Language, literature and area studies	7.39	(59)
Other arts	5.61	(63)

This gives a somewhat different picture from a simple count of numbers of publications quoted by Startup. Simple counts favour subject areas (such as science) which tend towards greater numbers of shorter journal papers, over other areas (eg, within arts) where the common currency is often the single-authored book. The relative weighting of different forms of publication in an index is obviously a subject which would be open to intense debate.

Halsey (1992) has some interesting figures showing differing emphases between what were the British universities and polytechnics; these are given in Table 6.4.

Table 6.4 *Trends in research output, 1976 and 1989*

	1976		1989	
	University	Polytechnic	University	Polytechnic
Currently engaged on research expected to lead to publication (%)	93	60	95	71
No papers ever published (%)	12	50	3	27
20 or more papers published (%)	26	2	53	10
Academic books published (mean)	0.8	0.3	2.4	0.7
Publications in last two years (mean)	3.5	0.9	6.3	2.0
No publications in last two years (%)	23	68	9	46

Source: Halsey, 1992, p. 187.

Differences between the universities and former polytechnics can clearly be seen with respect to expectations regarding the conduct of research leading to publication. However, the increase in publication activity within the polytechnics during this period is one of the features of the table.

But publication increased in the universities too, leading to some interesting information. For example, Halsey reports that in 1964 more than two thirds of university staff had never published a book, whereas by 1989 this figure had fallen to 42 per cent. He also makes some comment on the association between research productivity and promotion to the rank of professor:

> A person who has published over twenty articles is eight times more likely to be found among the professors than a person who has published less than ten articles. Between ten and twenty articles gives twice the chance of becoming a professor as publishing less than ten. Each book increases the odds on being a professor by 0.43; thus three books more than double the odds (Halsey, 1992, p. 207).

It is perhaps worth pointing out that although Startup's sample of university staff was quite small and restricted, his figure of 46 per cent publishing *more than* 20 papers appears to be quite close to Halsey's figure of 53 per cent publishing 20 *or more*. This might lend some credibility to the figures.

Number and value of research grants and contracts

Many of the factors mentioned already apply to the assessment of applications for research grants. The make-up of the reviewing committee is of importance, and there is no guarantee that the decisions made would be vindicated by a committee comprising different individuals. Cole *et al.* (1981), for example, sent 150 grant applications to a new set of referees and found that the amount of agreement between these and the original referees was mid-way between complete agreement and what could be expected simply through chance.

There are also connections between publication and the award of research grants. The funding of a research project obviously increases the chances of the applicant publishing, and is itself influenced by the publication record or success in winning research funding of the applicant in the past. What is currently fashionable in research, what is currently deemed to be socially valuable, what may have direct economic or similar applied potential, can lead to the funding of some applications and the rejection of others. Those rejected might well be of equal or greater quality in terms of academic or theoretical criteria.

How can I evaluate my research and publications?

These then are some of the ways in which research and publication are evaluated, and some of the problems which may be encountered in the process. So what can the individual do to try to gauge his or her own research and publication position? In order to approach this question, it is useful to think again of the categories we employed earlier in looking at teaching.

Your own research and publication record will be evaluated, perhaps adequately, perhaps not, for *institutional* purposes such as tenure, promotion or application for leave. This kind of evaluation will usually be 'backward looking' and judgemental, or what educationalists call 'summative evaluation'. On the other hand your research can also be evaluated for *developmental* purposes. This is usually more 'forward looking' and non-judgemental, in that your experience of research and publication so far is seen as giving background and a context from which to illuminate *possibilities* concerning your direction and plans for the future.

Evaluation of your research for institutional purposes focuses mainly on *products*. It is often concerned with your publications, perhaps your citations, and the reviews your publications have attracted. It is conducted mainly by others, such as members of promotions committees and, under some appraisal systems, the head of department.

Evaluation for development, on the other hand, tends towards *processes*. The importance here is for self-understanding: for you to gain a greater understanding of how you have arrived at your present position, and where you intend to go in the future. You are the principal in this process, although you may ask other people such as colleagues, fellow workers in the field, or the head of department, to give you their own perspectives on your work.

Institutional appraisal systems often combine elements of judgemental/product-oriented assessment, and developmental/process-oriented monitoring and evaluation. I should reiterate that the position taken in this book is that it is for you to decide how far you wish to take the insights you gain through looking at your own research and publication position into the formal appraisal system at your institution. We will certainly cover both aspects as we pose a number of questions in the remainder of this chapter. We will start with the institutional perspective and then move towards the developmental one. The developmental aspect is taken further in the next chapter of this book.

- *Where do I stand with regard to evaluating and documenting my research and publication record? What information can I present for institutional evaluation purposes such as tenure, promotion or appraisal?*

One way to approach these questions is to take a new look at your cv. The cv is the usual way in which we present a digest of our research and publication activities to date. You might want to make a copy of your cv and to put yourself in the place of someone (eg, a promotions committee member) attempting to understand and evaluate your research and publication record from your cv. That could well raise some interesting questions for you.

For example, how current is your cv? Do you have different versions of it for different purposes? How is your cv organized? Is it organized according to the guidelines which your institution suggests for promotion applications or for appraisal? Within these guidelines (allowing for a little flexibility), have you been able to offer any explanations or interpretations of your research and publication activities? Does the part of your cv covering research and publication simply have a list of publications, or have you briefly commented on and explained the purpose and direction of your research, or changes of direction you have made? Bearing in mind the material presented earlier in this section (eg, the type of publication normal in your field, number of authors) is there anything you wish to mention about the specific context in which you work?

- *What is my pattern of research and publication to date?*

In explaining the direction, changes of direction, purpose or purposes of your research so far, you should carefully examine your publications. How has the topic (or topics) of your research developed or changed and for what reasons? Look at the kinds of publications you have produced and are now producing. Is there any pattern here? For example, a fairly common pattern of progression might see you starting off by delivering a paper which was published in conference proceedings. You might then have submitted a smallish paper to a lesser journal in the hope of getting it published – *anywhere*. Next you might have published a number of smallish papers in lesser journals, in an attempt to boost your cv for such reasons as renewal of a contract, tenure or promotion. Given security of tenure, the pattern might then have shifted towards more substantial papers, perhaps review-type papers, taking longer to produce and written with more prestigious journals in mind. Next, and as your name became more widely known, you might have been invited to contribute a chapter to an edited book, and then another. This could have encouraged you to think about editing or writing a book yourself.

   Although this might be a fairly common kind of progression, it is not intended as a plan of action. It is offered as no more than an example of the kind of pattern which you may be able to discern from your own record of publication. Some people start by writing a book (eg, based on their PhDs), some people start by contributing to multi-authored papers, others by writing alone. What path can you discern through your own publication activities and how can you explain this? How does your own pattern compare with others in your area? What makes your pattern different from the norm and do you see this as a strength or a weakness? With whom might you discuss all of this?

- *Which referees can I call on?*

If you are making a case for promotion or tenure, do you have access to the comments of your head of department or dean? Have you fully explained the direction, changes of direction and pattern of your research and publication career to this person? Have you given him or her copies of reviews, citation information or other material which could be of use in writing a document to support your case? Have you discussed this with the person and pointed out what you consider to be the main elements and strengths of your research and publication record? Are you allowed to nominate referees of your own? Who will these be; have you considered this question carefully and sought their prior agreement?

- *Where do I stand currently with regard to my research project(s)?*

Whether you have a number of research projects on the go at the moment, or just one, consider each and describe the point you think you have reached. When do you plan to have the project completed and what vehicle (journal, etc) have you identified for publication? How realistic are your plans on both counts (time and vehicle)? Is there anyone with whom you can talk over these plans; anyone whose opinion you respect, who has been through a similar process him or herself, and who could give another perspective on your plans? Do you have any contingency plans should the project(s) take longer than you estimate, or for re-submission of the publication if it is rejected by your first-choice journal or publisher?

- *What do I want to say in the appraisal interview about my research to date?*

Do the appraisal forms you have to fill in allow you to not only list your publications, but to adequately interpret your research direction, problems and achievements? Do you need to supplement the forms by writing a paragraph or two in order to explain your position? If you do not wish to write anything, what do you want to say in order to explain and interpret the information required on the appraisal forms? How far do you wish to share with the appraiser any insights you might have gained into your past and present pattern of research? Are there any questions concerning research which you would like to ask the appraiser? Are you adequately prepared in this area for your appraisal interview?

Notes

1 A recent publication which may be useful to those who find themselves in reorganized and renamed institutions which now require them to make a research commitment is Kate Beattie's (1993) *So Where's your Research Profile? A Resource Book for Academics.* Aimed at staff in Australia's former Colleges of Advanced Education (now universities) it contains material which may be of more general interest and use.
2 An alternative position is taken by Ernest Boyer (1990) in *Scholarship Reconsidered.* He locates academic pursuits within the notion of scholarship, designating different forms of scholarship variously as discovery, integration, application and teaching.

Chapter Seven

Where am I going with my research?

Introduction

In this chapter we look to the future in terms of your research and publication activities. From the previous chapter you may have started to develop a somewhat clearer understanding of where you stand with regard to these activities at the moment. You may also have begun to think more systematically about where you intend the research and publication side of your career to go in the future. Towards the end of this chapter you will be invited to flesh out some of your thoughts in more detail, but before you do this, I will attempt to open up some areas of context which could influence how you see your plans for research in the future.

Research in the context of career

The researcher's life-cycle

In the previous chapter you made a start on trying to understand, interpret and find a pattern for your research and publication activities. We will now attempt to take this a little further. There are as many stories to be told about the way the research and publication aspect of an academic's career has developed as there are academics to tell them. This having been said, it is still possible to argue that a number of general stages can be traced in what might be called the 'life-cycle' of a researcher, which many academics share in common. Tony Becher (1989) describes three such stages: the achievement of independence; the mid-life crisis; the end-point of active research. I will briefly describe each of Becher's stages in turn.

Achieving independence

For many academics there is a stage prior to their gaining 'fully-fledged' academic status. Doctoral students and post-doctoral research fellows are especially prone to this experience. They cannot supervise research students nor apply for grants under their own names. Despite this, it can be a time of great importance, as directions taken now may well determine the development of a whole career. For example, Ziman (1981) states that 50 per cent of the last 100 Fellows of the Royal Society to die had stayed with the same speciality all their lives: 'That is to say, it was even money that a scientist whose PhD thesis or first published paper had been on, say, marine worms, would die as the world's most eminent authority on marine worms' (p. 16).

Research on eminent scholars does not always generalize to the majority, and even eminent scholars change specialism. The point remains, however, that at the beginning of one's 'life-cycle' in research, there are difficult questions to face with regard to:

- staying with a known approach, or starting off in a different direction;
- staying with a supervisor or research team, or departing;
- going for a large problem which may take several years, or for smaller projects capable of being finished more quickly;
- going for a popular area where there is much activity, or for a more peripheral area, where there is less.

Some of these choices offer greater security than others, but as with most things in life, it is usually the case that the larger the gamble, the greater the potential pay-off. Difficult and pressing choices such as these typically face us as we endeavour to achieve our independence and establish a position for ourselves as academics.

The mid-life crisis

Often occurring in our late 30s or early 40s, the mid-life (or mid-career) crisis is described by Becher as being concerned with 'whether or not to continue working within the same specialism, whether to switch to another one, or whether to begin the process of moving away altogether from active research' (p. 114). A change of specialism is obviously something which is not undertaken lightly, as it could well have taken many years to gain the knowledge, understanding, language or technical skill associated with a particular area. New networks of contacts, a new reputation, and credibility with funding agencies may also need to be established.

In science, the techniques learned as a research student might be exploited for as long as 10 or 15 years, but eventually they are superseded. In areas of the social sciences and humanities, differing perspectives and insights gain favour. For example, positivism (and quantitative methods), phenomenology (and qualitative methods), critical theory and post-structuralism have each made an impression. Sometimes the move from one area to another is abrupt; sometimes quite gradual, as 'to avoid a complete hiatus in one's publications, it [is] important to continue some writing in the field one [is] leaving while gearing up to contribute to the literature of the new affiliation' (Becher, 1989, p. 117). Sometimes the movement is to a discipline next door, sometimes to one some distance away. But irrespective of the size or scope of the move, Becher contends that it is far more prevalent than has often been thought (remember the marine worms?), and is 'among the most potent sources of innovation and development within a discipline' (p. 118). In science especially, being able to attend an important international conference, or to take sabbatical leave at an institution where new techniques may be learned, can be of crucial importance in coping with mid-career hiatus.

The end-point of active research

Apart from a shift of area, another distinct possibility associated with the mid-life crisis is for research to be abandoned. Again, Becher found a number of explanations, rationalizations (and indictments) for this, including:

- increased administrative load at departmental or university level;
- office-bearing or responsibility in a professional association or society;
- movement towards more reflective, theoretical or synoptic work;
- failure to rethink a problem or retool a lab;
- leaving academic life altogether;
- concentration on undergraduate teaching.

Interestingly, the last reason was the most common of all. And as to the phenomenon of burn-out, Becher found only limited support, and that mainly in mathematics or theoretical physics. In other words, there are very productive elderly researchers in all disciplines, and experience counts for a lot. Although there is conflicting evidence concerning the age at which people are most productive in different disciplines (Fox, 1983), it certainly appears that, in Becher's memorable phrase: 'if custom has the scope to stale, yet age must lack the power to wither the propensity for intellectual excellence' (p. 122).

Whose life-cycle? Women, men and research

The 'life-cycle' analogy is an attempt to find some pattern or similarity in academic careers, especially with regard to research. It may not hold for many men, and could be even less applicable to women. The sample taken by Halsey (1992) provided the data shown in Table 7.1 with respect to differences between women and men in academia.

Table 7.1 *Women and men in higher education in Great Britain, 1989*

	Women	Men
Age (mean years)	43.5	46.4
Marital status (%)		
Married or living as married	68.2	86.7
Separated/Divorced/Widowed	13.6	6.1
Never married	18.2	7.2
Subject area (%)		
Arts	24.7	15.3
Social Sciences	41.3	27.5
Natural Sciences	13.5	28.2
Engineering/Technology	3.7	15.6
Medicine/Health	16.0	11.6
Agriculture/Forestry/Veterinary	0.9	1.8
Rank (%)		
Professor	3.9	15.3
Reader/Senior or Principal lecturer	38.1	42.2
Lecturer	58.0	42.5
Terms of Employment (%)		
Full-time	92.7	96.0
Part-time	7.3	4.0
Contract terms (%)		
To retirement	67.4	79.0
No specific time	16.4	11.7
Fixed term	12.7	5.4
Probationary	3.2	2.4
Other	0.2	1.5
Research orientation (%)		
Mainly research	20.5	27.8
Research and teaching	27.5	28.7
Mainly teaching	52.1	43.3
Allocation of time (%)		
Teaching undergraduates	35.2	33.1
Doing research	20.8	23.2
Insufficient time for research because of teaching	81.8	64.3
Supervision of research students (%)	47.1	59.7
Publications		
20 or more articles (%)	21.0	43.3
Number of books (mean)	2.3	2.3

Source: Halsey, 1992, pp. 224, 228 and 232, based on a sample number of 1861 men and 298 women.

According to Halsey's data, women tend to be less research-oriented and more teaching-oriented than men. Women tend to be more engaged in the teaching of undergraduates, less in the supervision of postgraduates and to have less time for research because of teaching, than do men. Women also tend to be more likely to experience poorer employment terms and to be in the position of 'secondary bread-winner'. They are more likely to experience career breaks (for childbirth and care) and to have their careers jeopardized by their husbands' career movements (Halsey, 1992, p. 226).

The fact that women have less satisfactory employment terms and tend to be less engaged in research, may probably be interpreted as both cause *and* effect with regard to promotion and the decline which is observed in the number of women higher up the career ladder.

We should not view all of this as static and unchangeable. There have been real gains made in participation rates for women as students at the undergraduate level and more modest gains in participation rates for women as faculty staff. The last place to feel the impact has been among the ranks of senior academic managers and decision makers. Patterns of childcare are changing too, and the flexibility of employment which many academics still enjoy makes it easier for men to take major responsibility, or a fairer share, in this aspect of family life.

What has all of this got to do with research? It is for each of us to plan, negotiate and stumble our way towards a (shifting) reconciliation of the place which research and publication will occupy in our lives. Life-cycles and stereotypes may give us some insights concerning what *can* happen, but they do not prescribe what *will* happen. It is important for each of us, and especially important for women, to take full account of the vital link which continues to exist between research and promotion, as we attempt to plan our careers.[1]

Making time for research

We have already gone through a number of questions concerning whether you consider yourself to be primarily a teacher or a researcher, and what proportion of time you think it appropriate to allocate to these activities. Just as there is some aggregate information with regard to teaching, there is also similar information concerning research. For example, Halsey (1992) quotes the figures shown in Table 7.2.

Table 7.2 *Actual and ideal proportions of working time spent on research and administration (%), 1989*

Activity	University		Polytechnic	
	Actual	*Ideal*	*Actual*	*Ideal*
Research and other creative activity	28	43	15	30
Administration, management (examining, committees, admissions, etc)	24	12	28	16

Source: Halsey, 1992, p. 186.

If we compare the data in Table 7.2 with those in Table 5.1 (see p. 65) we can see that whereas the figures with respect to teaching showed the actual and ideal proportions of working time to be fairly similar, when it comes to research and administration there are marked differences. Staff in the former polytechnics said that the time they could spend in research was only about half of that for staff in the universities. Both university and former polytechnic staff wanted to spend a much greater percentage of their time doing research than they were able to. Also, both sets of staff wanted to cut the proportion of the time they spent in administration by about half.

When Halsey asked about handicaps to research, university staff identified 'other commitments' as being more important than teaching commitments, whereas former polytechnic staff saw these as being equally important. This reflects the larger teaching workloads in the former polytechnics. Indeed, 44 per cent of former polytechnic staff said that the research they could do during term time was 'almost none', as can be seen in Table 7.3.

Table 7.3 *Handicaps to research (%)*

	1976		1989	
	University	Polytechnic	University	Polytechnic
Obstacle to research is:				
1. teaching commitments	36	65	57	77
2. other commitments			76	77
Research during term				
substantial			27	13
little			49	43
almost none			24	44

Source: Halsey, 1992, p. 188.

In terms of the 'normal' activities of an academic, therefore, it seems that research is the one which tends to be squeezed out, the activity which academics say they need more time for, and from the information presented in the last chapter, the activity which tends to be kept up *not* at the expense of teaching, but to the detriment of family, friends and social life. Many of us have our own personal experience of this.

Becher (1989) also found that administration, committee work and marking were held to be the more unsatisfactory facets of academic life while teaching was 'generally held to be enjoyable and worthwhile' (p. 123). To do research, however, one had to be 'dedicated and determined', 'monomaniac' and 'obsessed'. This was truer in what Becher (I think mistakenly) calls the 'hard knowledge areas', but even here there were dissenting voices, and those who thought it essential to '"know when you have to stop working"', and to avoid too much emotional intensity by the deliberate cultivation of other interests' (p. 123). There was less talk of obsession in the 'softer knowledge areas' and seemingly a better integration of 'work' and 'life'. Even so, finding time for research and integrating it satisfactorily into our lives as academics is an enduring problem for many of us.

Where am I going with my research? The case studies

Once more, as a way of easing into considering your own plans with regard to research and publication, it might be useful to spend a little time looking at some of the case studies which were introduced earlier.

BARBARA (BRIAN) LANGTON

Summary reminder. Barbara Langton is a relative newcomer to lecturing and will soon be facing a decision on tenure. She has had a very heavy teaching load, reorganizing and developing a number of courses. She has not published anything significant since joining the department, nor has she had the time to seek research funding.

When I took the time to look at my career, I saw danger signals with regard to having my appointment confirmed, and I realized how important it is for me to get going with research and to publish. I have decided that I need to restore a balance to my work between teaching and research, where in the past I have concentrated on teaching. I really believe that the department needed me to do this, but I now have to look to my own interests and my future career prospects.

My immediate career objectives now are to concentrate on research, certainly until I have tenure. I was actually promised reasonable set-up and equipment funds from the department when I joined but these have not come through. Part of that may be my fault in that I have not pressed for them – I was too busy teaching! Some other people in the department have post-doctoral fellows working for them too, but this has never been raised as a possibility with me. Taking all these things into account, I will devise a two-year action plan and set myself some objectives. What this means in nitty-gritty terms is that I will do these things:

- Immediately set about writing up for publication the research I did for my postgraduate degree. There is enough there for at least two papers, it's just that I have not had the time to look at it since I started teaching. This will be my first task and I will attack it vigorously.
- Go to at least one international and one local conference a year over the next two years and present papers which will appear in proceedings. I have neglected going to conferences in the struggle to keep my head above water with my teaching. I have a couple of ideas for things I could present and I will make the effort to do this. Having deadlines to meet will help me get the papers finished, and these conference proceedings papers will keep my publications ticking over.
- Start looking at making a research grant application. I think I might be able to work with some other people in the department who have longish-term programmes and grants, and this might give me a good angle for some funding. I need to establish something to keep me going after I write up the stuff that I already have.

- Talk this over in the appraisal interview and ask for some relaxation of the teaching I have been doing so that I can spend more time on research. This means that I will have to hand back some of the courses I have taken on, but that can't be helped. I will look for financial support in presenting the conference papers, revisit the set-up and equipment funding which I never received and discuss the possibility of taking on a post-doctoral fellow or graduate students. I will also ask for advice concerning how I could work with other people in developing the research grant application.

MICHAEL (MICHELLE) RICHARDS

Summary reminder. Michael Richards is also a relatively new lecturer coming up for tenure. He has previous commercial and industrial experience but is enjoying the flexibility of an academic position. He has not had much to do with other people in the department. Michael has nearly completed a PhD; he published a couple of papers last year and has considerable PhD research material remaining. He has recently had a poor student evaluation of his teaching.

In terms of research I can see that I am nearing the end of one cycle and that I need to start things moving towards the next. I certainly need to finish off my PhD and to make sure I capitalize on it in terms of papers. At the same time I also need to look to the future when my appointment has been confirmed, and what I will be doing for research and publication then. Taking these things into account, my objectives are something like this:

- I will have a finished and final copy of my PhD in six weeks time (eight weeks at the outside).
- I will make sure that I continue to mine my research data as I have been doing and produce another four or so papers before the final decision on tenure is made.
- I will carry on with planning the project with my colleague in the commercial world with a view to submitting a proposal for funding of this applied research by the end of next term. Included in the proposal will be funding for two graduate research students. I will make sure that I have cleared the ground (and approached some people) with regard to resources (space and some equipment) so that we can get going straight away if the funding comes through.

JANET (JOHN) SMITH

Summary reminder. Janet Smith has tenure and has published very successfully. She has had good student evaluations of her lectures, less so of her tutorials. She is very forceful in committee work. Janet is ambitious to advance and is frustrated that she is not advancing quickly enough. She is beginning to think about moving elsewhere.

My new book is going well and I have a good idea for my next book project. In terms of research, I think I just need to keep doing more of the same. My objectives are pretty clear:

- Finish the book in six months' time, which is slightly before the contract deadline. This means keeping to the scheme of work I have, and continuing to be ruthless in allocating myself my set 'writing times' during the week, evenings and weekends. I have also planned to spend a three-week stretch during the vacation in a library some distance away where I need to finish up on some documentary research and reading.

- Next month would be a good time to put together a proposal for the next book. I might as well get this in soon, as it seems to take an inordinate amount of time to have proposals accepted. I know which publisher I want to approach, and I will do this informally at first, but then submit the proposal shortly afterwards. I have already asked them to send me a copy of the 'house rules' for book proposals, so I know what they are looking for. I might as well send off for the 'house rules' of the alternative publisher I have in mind so that I am ready, just in case things don't work out.

PAUL (PAULINE) WHITING

Summary reminder. *Paul Whiting has been a lecturer for many years and has been at the career grade for a considerable time but has never applied for promotion beyond it. He has a grown-up family and no thoughts of leaving the university. He has not published anything recently despite having plenty of ideas. He is very committed to and enthusiastic about teaching although he has never taken a student evaluation of his teaching. The HOD has raised the possibility that he might take over some of the appraisal interviews in the department next year.*

In thinking about where I am going with my career, it has become pretty clear that I have to make some decisions and set some objectives for the rest of my time up to retirement. I think it is unrealistic for me to pick up the kind of research I did earlier in my career, and it doesn't interest me that much now anyway. I am interested in the idea of students in my classes using computers to do some things, and I think I can turn this into a research project which I can publish. That shouldn't be too onerous, and leaves space for me to pick up on the other area I want to develop, which is that of playing a larger role in departmental administration. My objectives are therefore:

- Plan a new approach to one section of my course next year. The new approach will see the students using computers in order to consider some problems.
- Approach the educational development unit and see if someone there can advise me on how to go about this, and especially how to design the project, collect information, write it up and publish it. I might also approach a couple of colleagues in other departments who have done some things along similar lines.

CHARLES (CAROL) ROSS

Summary reminder. *Charles Ross is professor and head of department. He is heavily involved in both departmental and university-level administration. Charles retains a fairly full teaching load, but has not published much over the last ten years. He has also lost contact with the international research organization on which he once served. He is contemplating the prospect of retirement in a few years' time.*

The direction I have set myself with regard to my career is to be able to play a role after I retire. I realize it will be difficult to pick up the kind of research programme I was running some years ago and I am thinking instead of making a contribution in the area of strategic planning – looking at priorities for research and research funding in my area. I might also be able to employ my committee skills in this area too. I am keen on getting some extended leave when I shed my departmental responsibilities. In order to move forward in this direction I need to do the following things:

- Change the direction of my efforts so that they are in line with the rationale I decided earlier in planning my future career.
- I will re-establish contact with people at both the national and international levels of the associations with which I used to be involved. Some are old friends and there will be no difficulty, others I know of and I will make it my business to get to know them. I will let it be known that I am back on the scene and ready to take on responsibilities. I will start contacting people soon, and there is a local conference this year and an international conference next year, where I can take this further.
- Make a formal request for extended leave after I have completed the hand-over of the headship. I have informal agreement for this leave, but I now need to firm this up and present the rationale and details of the programme I intend to pursue during this leave.
- Apart from contacting and talking to people, I will pick up on reading and familiarizing myself with what has been happening in terms of strategic research planning in my area. It would be good if I could write perhaps a couple of papers in this area over the next year or so. It is a bit vague at the moment, but I should start to see things more clearly when I get into the material.

Your turn

Now it is your turn to think about and make some plans regarding research and publication. As before, it is a good idea for you to make notes as you consider the questions which follow. It would also be a good idea for you to have your diary and year planner (or computer calendar and planner) available while you work through the questions.

- *How do I see research and publication in terms of my overall career development in the future?*

How important is research and publishing in the overall context of your career at the moment? Has it become more or less important than it was? Why? What role do you think research and publication will play in the development of your career in the future?

If you were to choose how you would allocate percentages of your time with regard to teaching, research, administration, etc, how would you do this; what would the figures be? (You may have done this already when you considered teaching. If so, would you wish to change the figures after completing the chapters on research?) What do the figures tell you about the place you think research and publication should presently occupy in your career, and about the way you actually allocate your time?

- *How can I make time for research and publication?*

What actual amount of time can you see yourself allocating for research? Have you allowed for this by allocating time in your diary and year planner and by making semester, term, weekly or daily plans? How does the amount of time you spend on research compare with other people you know?

Have you allocated time for monitoring, reflecting upon and evaluating the research and publication objectives you have set yourself? Are there developmental activities you need to pursue to help with your research or writing? For example, do you need to acquire new knowledge, new skills, learn a new procedure, learn to word-process, use bibliographic software, qualitative software, a new statistical procedure, etc? Can you plan to do this now, to set aside time in your diary when you can undertake this activity and so develop your research skills for the future?

- *Where am I going with my research and publications?*

Recap the previous chapter where you took a new look at your cv, evaluated your publication record and looked for a pattern in what, where and how you have published. What is the relationship between the pattern of your research and publications so far, and your intentions for the future? What similarities are there, what differences? Are there any alternatives you can think of in terms of the future direction of your research? If you are convinced of the direction you are following, are there any alternative options as to how to get there? In either case, what are the alternatives and what are the pros and cons?

Are you reaching the end of an 'era' in terms of your research, or is there still much left for you to do in your present area? Do you see yourself taking on new projects in much the same vein as your present projects, or branching out into a somewhat different area? Is there a likelihood of change in terms of:

- topics or areas of research;
- methods, approaches, techniques;
- products (multi- or single-authored; magazine or newspaper articles, book reviews; short journal papers; long papers, review papers; chapters in books; editing your own book; writing your own book; prestige of journals or publishers).

- *Can I make some specific plans regarding research and publication projects?*

Just as you did in the previous chapter with regard to your *present* research, try to list your plans for research and publication projects in the *future*. Outline when you intend to start the project, when it should be completed and what vehicle (journal, etc) you think will be appropriate for publication. How realistic are your plans on both counts (time and vehicle)? Do you have any contingency plans should the project(s) take longer than you estimate, or for re-submission of the publication if it is rejected by your first-choice journal or publisher?

- *What support can I gather?*

Is there anyone with whom you can talk over your plans; anyone whose opinion you respect, who has been through a similar process him or herself, and who could give another perspective on your plans? If you are just starting out or wanting to make a start on research, are there others in the department who are in a similar position? Your possible areas of research may not be identical but you could still form a small support group in which you could share your experiences of getting started, the difficulties you have faced and how these can be overcome. Could you approach your HOD for support in this?

- *What research responsibilities do I have towards others?*

Do you have responsibilities for others engaged with you in research? Do you have colleagues, research students, post-docs, technicians or others who are intimately bound up in your research programme and dependent on it? How do you see the future for each of these people? What are the likely consequences for them of the plans you are making? Is there anything that you can do now to help them adjust, help them gain new skills or knowledge which they will need, allow them more autonomy or give them more responsibility in particular areas?

- *What is my action plan for research and publication?*

Having worked through the questions above, can you now draw together some of the insights you have gained, set priorities and decide on an action plan? It will help to make the objectives you set yourself as clear as possible, and to have a good idea of how you can assess if the objective has been met successfully. Think back to the case studies earlier in this section. Barbara Langton set herself clear objectives concerning the number of papers she will write up from her PhD, the number of papers she will present at national and international conferences, and the way she will go about making an application for a research grant. Janet Smith had clear time allocations which will allow her to finish the book she is presently writing, and start the proposal process for the next one.

Bear in mind when you are making your action plan that you do not set yourself too many objectives, that they are realistic and attainable (but still challenging), and that you specify a timetable of events. This last point means that you plan for and decide when you will begin, how long you will proceed before taking stock (monitoring and evaluating), and when you intend to finish.

You should also consider who can help you, or to whom you can talk about your plans. Being able to talk over some ideas and plans with a trusted colleague can not only give you important reinforcement and encouragement, but someone approaching it from a different viewpoint can sometimes come up with very worthwhile suggestions.

● *What about the appraisal interview?*

How far do you wish to disclose your long- and short-term objectives and plans in the appraisal interview? What will be your stance towards research and publication in the interview; what do you wish to discuss; what objectives and plans will you put forward? Do you need to supplement the appraisal forms by writing a short note which explains and justifies your position? If not, have you worked out anyway what you want to say to the appraiser in order to explain and interpret the direction you are taking? What do you anticipate will be your appraiser's attitude towards your research and publication plans? Is it likely that he or she will be positive and encouraging, or negative? Do you wish to bring up any matters concerning resources, funding, space, equipment, materials, other support, training or development for research and publication? Make a careful note of exactly what you will ask for and how you can justify each request you make.

Summary

In drawing up an action plan concerning where you are going with your research and publishing, you might consider the following points:

● Long-term objectives for both your research *and* your publishing.
● Short-term objectives (ie, next year) for your research *and* your publishing.
● How will these objectives be met; what are your plans?
● What is the time-frame for achieving your objectives (from start, to monitoring, to completion).
● Who can help or assist you, to whom can you talk?
● How will you monitor the process, judge if you are making progress?
● How will you evaluate how successful you have been in meeting your objectives; how will you know?

Note

1 For further reading on women's experience of (mainly American) academia see Aisenberg and Harrington (1988), Simeone (1987), Theodore (1986), and Welch (1990).

Chapter Eight

What about my other responsibilities?

Introduction

As academics, we take on other responsibilities and tasks apart from those directly related to our teaching and research. In fact, academics collectively take on an astonishingly wide range of responsibilities and tasks in addition to teaching and research.

There is, of course, an obvious need for administration (or management) in order that a framework be provided within which decisions can be made concerning priorities and resources. It is generally recognized by academics that administration, at one level or another, will form part of their everyday lives. But it has always been recognized too that institutions of higher education have a wider role to play within the community. Much of this is assumed within a conception of service, which is often linked with public service or service to the local community. Here is another area in which we might be involved.

The responsibilities of academics also reach into other areas. Most academics would claim to have subject area or discipline loyalties and responsibilities, which encourage them to be involved in academic societies or professional institutes. They recognize a separate responsibility towards their disciplines, quite apart from responsibility towards a local institution or local community. Apart from involvement in an academic society or professional institute, this responsibility towards a subject area or discipline may also persuade them to deliver papers to a variety of groups and institutions, to be involved in a research council, or to take on various duties associated with external examining.

These are just some of the ways in which academics make contributions other than by direct participation in teaching and research within their own institutions. In this chapter we will look at areas such as these before considering how the people introduced earlier as case studies might explain their own involvements. It will then be your turn to map out the areas in which you are personally involved, to evaluate where you stand presently with respect to these areas and to consider where you are going in the future.

Areas of responsibility

Any categorization of this diffuse topic is bound to be problematic. A certain amount of blurring between the categories is inevitable and some people will claim quite legitimately that the categories hold little relevance for them. Be that as it may, what follows is an attempt to order our 'other responsibilities' by defining them within the three categories of: administration, external academic work and external earnings.

Administration

We have already seen in the previous chapter how university staff spend about a quarter of their working time in administration and how, ideally, they would wish to cut this proportion by about half (Halsey, 1992, p.186). Let us now look a little more closely at what is entailed in administration.

Normal administrative duties
The first level of administration for most of us is administration associated with our own teaching and research. This might include such things as setting exam papers, marking assignments, organizing the printing of a laboratory manual, ordering textbooks, making restricted access material available at the library, booking tutorial or laboratory rooms, etc. It also includes writing references for students. I will not elaborate this aspect of administration, preferring instead to consider it as part and parcel of the normal business of teaching and research, or the normal administrative duties of an academic. You may wish to look at routine administration such as this when you consider your own teaching and research. It may well be that changes to administrative procedure go hand in glove with the evaluation you make of where you presently stand and what your plans are for the future.

Departmental administrative duties
The first set of administrative duties I will consider are those at departmental (or similar) level. Here, you are responsible not only for yourself and your course, but also to 'others'. The 'others' may be the whole department or, for example, a course team. Some examples of the kinds of role you might play (for a particular course or for the whole department) are as follows:

- Admissions coordinator.
- Examinations coordinator.

- Coordinator of tutors or demonstrators (perhaps responsible for selecting, training and monitoring tutors).
- Responsibility for general, technical or laboratory members of staff.
- Coordinator of textbook ordering.
- Coordinator or departmental representative for room allocations.
- Coordinator for electives, field placements, industrial or commercial placements, an exchange programme.
- Programme or departmental link person with another institution (eg, local college).
- Departmental publicity coordinator, departmental newsletter editor.
- Responsibility for contacts with former students, departmental representative on former students' association.
- Departmental representative on the university computer users group, library committee, staff development committee or other faculty or university-level committees.

Head of department

The major responsibility for departmental administration is taken by the head of department. The role of the HOD has possibly never been more contentious than it is at present, with different viewpoints arguing for different definitions of the head's proper function. The polarities of this debate often pit collegiality against managerialism. The collegial model looks back to the collegiate of Oxford where academics governed themselves and their colleges democratically. The alternative (and predominant) form of government found in Germany, France and the USA tended to be more monolithic, bureaucratic and hierarchical, with segmentation taking place along departmental lines (Halsey, 1992, p.156).

The role of the HOD in the collegial model is seen as being that of 'chairperson' and facilitator, with executive and administrative decisions being subjected to the will of the department as a whole. Members of the department are colleagues and peers, professionals and equals who are willing to entrust responsibility to the HOD, so long as he or she acts in a responsible manner and seeks their mandate. Conversely, the hierarchical model in its most recent guise sees the HOD as managing director. He or she is appointed to make decisions, to control and to manage the department, irrespective of the popularity of particular measures taken. Indeed, difficult decisions need to be made, decisive management by committee is impossible and you can never please everyone. Because of this, responsibility should reside with the key decision maker, the HOD, who is seen as being essentially different from the rest of the staff: the 'line manager' in direct control of the department.

These are caricatures, of course, and many heads find ways to display strong leadership while at the same time managing to carry their colleagues along with them. But this begs the interesting question of *how* HODs know what response their leadership is receiving, or more generally, how HODs are evaluated. Heads are usually part of the appraisal process too, and can discuss their own career, teaching, research, administration or management plans with an appraiser, often a dean, assistant vice chancellor or similar. But what data do they bring to this discussion, apart from the teaching and research information which we have already discussed? How do they evaluate where they stand presently, as a precursor to outlining how they see the department developing in the future? It is perhaps worth pursuing this matter a little further as it is of some interest to HODs, their appraisers and those who one day might become HODs. More generally than this, however, it is also of interest to ordinary members of staff who might reasonably expect appraisal to work not only from the top down, but also from the bottom up.

There are many resources available to HODs which spell out the research literature concerning what is entailed in the job, what is considered good practice and how evaluation may be approached.[1] On this latter point, two principles which have cropped up previously may be worthy of consideration once more. First, the greater the number and variety of sources of evidence which can be tapped, the more robust the evaluation. Second, the reason for the evaluation (for feedback or for institutional decision making) should be made clear.

There are certainly many people from whom HODs might invite comment. These include the head's appraiser (dean, assistant vice chancellor, etc), departmental academic staff, departmental general (support or technical) staff, post-doctoral fellows, postgraduate and undergraduate students, former students, peers (HODs) within the university and either inside or outside of the faculty, peers (HODs) outside the university but in similar positions, and outside interests which have an important relationship with the department (eg, industry groups taking release students, local branches of an institute, society or association, those at another institution with which the department has links). Of these, it is the task of gaining feedback information from academic staff *within* the department which is perhaps the most urgent, though surprisingly often neglected.

In order to gain such information, an HOD may arrange with the institution's educational development unit to construct a survey of staff opinion, and for the unit to analyse and provide frequencies of response for both rating scales (closed questions) and open-ended questions. The open-ended comments may be typed out in full for the HOD to consider in detail. When HODs undertake this kind of exercise, it is important that they prepare the ground well with their staff by explaining why they are asking for comment, and that they genuinely desire honest feedback on how they are performing, what they are seen to be doing well and where their performance could be improved. It is also useful for HODs to disseminate the main points to come out of the survey after they have had time to consider and discuss the results and, if necessary, reformulate plans for the future in light of the comments which they have received.

In Appendix VI are a number of rating scale and open-ended response items which an HOD might consider in drawing up such a survey. These have been adapted from the work of Ingrid Moses (see Note 1 at the end of this chapter). It is intended that this list be used as an aid. It is not necessary for HODs to use every item on the list, and it is highly desirable that they add further items concerning issues in which they are particularly interested, or which relate more closely to their own particular departmental context.

Higher level administrative duties

So far we have considered administrative tasks which individuals may undertake within a department, together with the person who forms the pinnacle of departmental responsibility: the head of department. The next hierarchical step in administration might be to faculty or divisional level, where departmental representation will often be required. Further on again, either departmental or faculty representation may be required at the level of university-wide committees, working parties or other similar mechanisms for the development and administration of university policy. Further still, groupings of universities (national and international) exist as, of course, do prestigious committees quite outside of the university sphere. For those who have shown an uncommon ability in committee work and administration there are thus further administrative outlets, and such people may find their talents in demand far beyond the confines of their own disciplines and their own universities.

External academic work

This category covers work of an academic nature which occurs outside of the normal institutional setting and which is usually either unpaid or rather poorly paid. Sometimes such work is viewed as part of a reciprocal responsibility: 'Yes, I will act as external examiner for your Masters student's thesis – you took on one of mine last year'. Here are some examples:

- Guest speaker at another university. This could include taking an undergraduate lecture or seminar, holding a seminar with postgraduate and research students, making a presentation for a departmental seminar series, or giving an open lecture or seminar.
- Guest speaker at a local group meeting. Covering a wide range of groups with particular interests, this could mean an historian, geographer, sociologist, anthropologist or linguist giving a talk to the local historical society; or a physiologist, surgeon, meteorologist, cartographer or marine ecologist giving a talk to the local diving club.
- Guest speaker at a local association meeting. This again covers many arrangements concerned with the link between school-level and tertiary activities. Local associations for the teaching of a particular subject can make quite considerable demands on the staff of a small university department, in terms of both administrative and academic contributions.

- The media. This could include writing an article for a local or national newspaper on a particular subject specialism or contributing to a radio or television programme on a particular subject. Most frequently it means taking part in a newspaper, radio or television interview.
- Making a conference presentation, giving an invited keynote address at a conference, acting as a paper or session discussant, acting as chair of a plenary session.
- External examining. Acting as external examiner for a particular academic or professional course or for external projects or theses. Such duties may be local and require little travel, or they may be national or international. Acting as an international external examiner tends to require a greater time commitment, especially in terms of travel, but also often offers high rewards in terms of prestige, personal development and service.
- Refereeing and publishing. This can vary from refereeing an occasional paper, to making the major time commitment which may be associated with editing a journal or taking responsibility for the desk-top publishing of a special interest group publication. Refereeing also extends to research grant applications and to the job applications of one's colleagues.
- Research councils and advisory committees. Apart from refereeing applications for research funding, academics also sit on research funding agencies, research councils and many advisory committees and bodies which bring together those with a special interest in a particular area. Such bodies may thus involve government, public and private sector interests and concerns.
- Involvement in an academic society or professional institute. As well as being an ordinary member and making presentations at the conferences of such groups, some academics take up opportunities which present themselves from time to time and become far more deeply involved. For example, this might mean taking a position of responsibility with regard to organizing a conference, or acting as a local branch representative or contact person. There are many other positions which require filling at both local (branch), national or international levels. These might include positions such as those of membership secretary, publications officer, chair of a special interest group, editor of a journal or ultimately, president of the society.

External earnings

External earnings have been somewhat dubiously distinguished from external academic work by the fact that they may be paid at a reasonable rate for the job. Just what constitutes 'reasonable' payment for such work is debatable. However, there is less likely to be an expectation of reciprocity from work primarily intended to provide external earnings than there is from external academic work. If the going rate is being paid, then reciprocity is less of a factor. Examples include the following:

- Consultancy. This includes a whole range of academic disciplines, from civil engineering to chemistry, psychology to accountancy, languages to statistics. Payment is made either directly to the person or team involved, or to an account of the university. There is usually a tax or some other incentive for taking the latter course, and monies thus earned can be used for such purposes as the purchase of new research equipment or the funding of conference or research-related travel.
- Extramural teaching. This again may take many forms, with perhaps the most common being teaching contracted by organizations such as the Open University, local technical colleges or adult education groups.

One of the main problems associated with consultancy is, who owns the problem? Where the research problem is decided by a client the position of the academic consultant can become difficult. The problem is in ensuring that the academic is '. . . left free to devote himself to whatever lines of inquiry he judges to be important . . .' (Startup, 1979, p. 91). On the other hand, Startup quotes university civil engineers engaged in consultancy as saying that:

> . . . a sharp division could not be drawn between research and consultancy work . . . a client would not approach a university based consultant with a routine problem and if the problem were not routine, it might well generate ideas and results which could form the basis of a published article (p.84).

So in some areas consultancy is seen as inseparable from research, whereas in others it is viewed as an inferior alternative. And there are somewhat similar arguments surrounding extramural teaching. There is no doubt that the pay we might earn from extramural teaching can be of vital importance to us in the early days of our careers. I am thinking here of a young academic, recently appointed and low on the lecturer scale, whose spouse has been unable to find a suitable job, and who has young children to support. Other professionals profit from their skills, so why not academics?

The danger is, of course, that in earning money through extramural teaching one may neglect other aspects of one's work, especially research and publication. But there can also be benefits to be gained from extramural teaching. An example of this might be that for the first time a young lecturer is faced with a combative group of mature students. They do not acquiesce easily to the lecturer's authority, they may be unwilling to take on trust the lecturer's position and usual explanations, and they will not allow their own failure to understand or grasp a point, to quietly slide by. Extramural teaching can afford opportunities for learning about teaching which may be infrequent during the normal course of higher education teaching, but which can enrich the understanding and skill of the teacher enormously.

With these thoughts in mind, let us now turn to the case study examples which were introduced earlier.

Other responsibilities: the case studies

BARBARA (BRIAN) LANGTON

Summary reminder. Barbara Langton is a relative newcomer to lecturing and will soon be facing a decision on tenure. She has had a very heavy teaching load, reorganizing and developing a number of courses. She has not published anything significant since joining the department, nor has she had the time to seek research funding. The objectives she has set for herself include finding a better balance between teaching and research by relinquishing some of her teaching, writing up papers from her postgraduate degree work, presenting papers at conferences, seeking equipment funding, making a research grant application and taking on a post-doctoral fellow or graduate students.

I have made a clear commitment towards research over the short term as my career is at greatest risk in this area. This means that in the year ahead I will not be keen to take on any additional administrative tasks. In fact, if all goes well and I hand over (or hand back!) some of my teaching to colleagues, I will be less caught up in course and examination administration than I have been previously.

It has been in the back of my mind for some time to take on some outside teaching at the local college. The courses I have developed and taught put me in a good position to do this, and I could certainly use the extra money. However, having taken a step back to look at my career generally, I now think that I will put this off, at least for the next year and possibly the year after that. By then I should be in a more comfortable position. I should have tenure, some papers published and a research programme up and running. I can look at taking on outside teaching then, if I am still interested. I will be in a better position to see if I want to take on other things which come along. At the moment, however, I do not want to lose the focus which I have somewhat painfully worked out for myself.

• Research is my clear focus for the next couple of years and as far as possible I want to avoid taking on administrative or extra teaching commitments.

MICHAEL (MICHELLE) RICHARDS

Summary reminder. Michael Richards is also a relatively new lecturer coming up for tenure. He has previous commercial and industrial experience but is enjoying the flexibility of an academic position. Michael has nearly completed a PhD; he published a couple of papers last year and has considerable PhD research material remaining. He has recently had a poor student evaluation of his teaching. Michael has committed himself to improving the student evaluations of teaching he receives, to finishing off his PhD and to continuing to publish from his PhD research material. In addition, he will submit a proposal for the funding of some applied research in conjunction with a colleague in the commercial world. The funding application will include provision for two postgraduate students.

The more I think about the research proposal I have been working on with my colleague in commerce, the more possibilities I see for it. Until I started looking systematically at my career it was no more than a vague possibility some years away in the future. Now I am in almost daily Email contact with my colleague and we see some very interesting possibilities for developments and spin-offs. We will have finished the funding application soon, including specification of the part to be played by the two postgraduate students. But my colleague has already picked up some interest from firms he works with about our project. It seems that there is a distinct possibility that we could be asked to act as consultants for a number of firms which are concerned about exactly the problem we are researching.

We don't want to rush the research or anticipate the outcome, but if things go well we could be offered some quite lucrative consultancies. This kind of money would really allow us to set up properly, with the latest equipment, and also to fund more research students. I can already think of a couple of areas where we could diversify the research, generalize and apply it in more areas. The money would come in handy here for getting us to the States to make personal contact with people working over there. I guess this might be counting chickens long before they are hatched, but the prospects are quite exciting.

On a more mundane note, I would like to become departmental representative on the university computer user's group. I have been very frustrated with the service we have been receiving from the central computer system and my efforts to have my concerns addressed have come to nothing. It seems that becoming departmental representative is not exactly a highly regarded honour (people run for cover whenever it comes up) so it should not be too difficult to get myself nominated.

- I will continue working on the joint research application but at an accelerated rate. We will investigate to see if we can tie down interest in our project with regard to the possibility of consultancies.
- I will try to have myself nominated as departmental representative on the computer user's group.

Janet (John) Smith

Summary reminder. Janet Smith has tenure and has published very successfully. She has had good student evaluations of her lectures, less so of her tutorials. She is very forceful in committee work. Janet is ambitious to advance and is frustrated that she is not advancing quickly enough. She is beginning to think about moving elsewhere. The objectives Janet has set herself include becoming a better facilitator in tutorials and committees, keeping to the deadline for delivery of the book she is writing and starting work towards a proposal for her next book.

I have tried to take a dispassionate look at the stage I have reached in my career. I am ambitious and eventually I want to become professor and head of department. I think I am doing everything right, but I seem to be progressing very slowly. That is why I am considering the possibility of moving on. In my present position it seems that I need to work on bridging the early part of my career (getting established, a name and reputation, etc) with how I see myself in the future. Essentially, this means doing what I can to further my international reputation. There are some things I can do about this.

First, I can look for more involvement in my professional society. In fact I have already chaired the local branch of the society, but I could think about holding office at a higher level. It is a prestigious international society, but I think I am well enough established and have a good enough reputation to try for publications officer: a job which includes the mundane chores associated with editing the society's journal. That would certainly do no harm to my international standing and would put me in regular contact with many of the major figures in the area. It could also serve as a useful springboard for higher office within the society in the years to come. No use being bashful, I would like to be president of the society one day.

Second, I could extend my role as external examiner. I have done some external work but it has been local and fairly *ad hoc*. I could let some of my colleagues know that I am interested in either national or international external examining, and see what happens from there.

Finally I need to consider the role that I see for myself *within* the university as long as I am here. I have not really made the transition yet from junior member of staff to the kind of person who has a name and is called upon to sit on faculty and university committees. Indeed, sometimes I think that I am better known internationally than I am in my own institution. It might have something to do with my manner in committees, but I have already decided to try and give myself more options and adopt a different approach there anyway. The crux is, if I am to become more involved within the university, what path will I take?

My friend Trevor pointed out the other day that as universities become more managerial, a devout careerist (me!) should prepare herself for advancement by establishing a record of administrative experience. Service on extra-departmental committees will count more highly than service on intra-departmental ones, and so extra-departmental involvement and experience is what I should be looking for. At the very least, I need to be careful about the kinds of administrative duties I take on at this stage, and try to ensure that they contribute towards my own career development plan.

- I will investigate the possibility of becoming publications officer (or holding some other office) in the international society.
- I will look for prestigious national or international external examination work.
- I will look for extra-departmental administrative responsibility by preference.

PAUL (PAULINE) WHITING

Summary reminder. Paul Whiting has been a lecturer for many years and has been at the career grade for a considerable time but has never applied for promotion beyond it. He has a grown-up family and no thoughts of leaving the university. He has not published anything recently despite having plenty of ideas. He is very committed to and enthusiastic about teaching although he has never taken a student evaluation of his teaching. The HOD has raised the possibility that he might take over some of the appraisal interviews in the department next year. Paul's objectives include evaluating his teaching for the first time and starting up a project using computers in the curriculum – to be written up for publication. He is also interested in taking on greater administrative responsibility within the department.

In looking at my career overall I have come to the conclusion that I have stalled and lost direction. For the past few years I have been simply 'carrying on' really without any thought about what I want to accomplish, what I want to do. Heaven knows I have been busy enough and it's not that I have been shirking, it's more that I have allowed myself to be carried along by the current, rather than paddling in a particular direction. This has all come as a bit of a revelation to me, but I am determined to make the most of the last part of my career, and to play a full and proper part in the affairs of the department.

One thing I want to start up right away is a departmental newsletter. I have been thinking about this for some time and it seems to me to be a good idea. As a department we seem to have less and less time these days to catch up with each other and to find out about what each of us is doing. The newsletter will keep people informed of what is going on in the department and of coming events. It will help to integrate the academic staff and general staff too, as everyone's news will be welcomed.

I know that I am pretty popular within the department and people talk to me easily (and a lot!). This should make the collection of items less of a chore. I also use humour in most things I do, and I should be able to use this to good advantage in keeping the newsletter 'light' and 'readable'. I could add in odd bits and pieces from the local paper, *The Times Higher* and things like that – even university memos (a perennial source of humour!). Technically it will be easy enough to produce as I can use my own word-processor to do it. I'll make a template with an eye-catching title or logo and use double column format.

I have definitely decided to take on the appraisal interviews (or staff development interviews, as we call them) which the HOD asked me to think about. I think I will be good at this as I seem to be able to empathize with people quite easily. However, I will go to the training sessions which are held for appraisers and also try to find out if there are other resources I should look at. Maybe there are some video tapes in the library. I will talk to colleagues in other departments too, to see what they have to say about the whole thing.

Finally, the position of admissions coordinator for postgraduate courses and degrees has to be filled as the person who was doing the job has left. I am on the committee and have been very frustrated with the procedure. It is all to do with trying to work out if previous qualifications and experience merit acceptance. We get people applying from all over the place and have to work out whether to accept them or not. We do not appear to have any clear guidelines (even after all this time) and far too often we seem to be constructing principles for admission, case by case. This often leads to inconsistencies and anomalies. The same kind of thing used to happen in our examinations committee with respect to the rounding up of marks. We sorted that out a couple of years ago, but the problems with admissions still remain. I think I will say to the HOD that I am willing to take on chairing the admissions committee and in that position try to develop some guidelines which will help us routinize our admissions procedure and cut down on the number of anomalies.

All in all I see myself taking more of a part in the functioning of the department. The idea that I could become head occurred to me earlier, and an interesting idea it is too. I will certainly keep it in mind as I look to get myself moving again, in a somewhat more directed way.

- I will ask people if they are interested in the idea of a departmental newsletter. If so, I will get it up and running.
- I will take on appraisal interviewing, go to the training sessions and try to find out how to do this well.
- I will offer to chair the postgraduate admissions committee and suggest changes with a view to smoothing its operation.
- I will try to take on responsibilities and a role within the department which could advance my prospects of becoming HOD. I will not be disappointed if nothing happens with respect to the headship, but I would like to put myself in a position where I could at least be considered (and consider it myself!).

CHARLES (CAROL) ROSS

Summary reminder. Charles Ross is professor and head of department. He is heavily involved in both departmental and university-level administration. Charles retains a fairly full teaching load, but has not published much over the last ten years. He has also lost contact with the international research organization on which he once served. He is contemplating the prospect of retirement in a few years' time. Charles has set himself the task of relinquishing both the headship and some of his university committee work. He intends to keep up his teaching commitments and to improve his tutorial arrangements. Charles also wishes to re-establish contact with former colleagues and to pursue an interest in strategic research planning. He hopes to continue to play a role in research committee work after he has retired.

It was in my mind to hand over headship of the department in a couple of years' time, but taking a systematic look at where I now stand and how little time I have until retirement has caused me to reconsider this. I now want to bring the hand-over forward, but at the same time to make it as smooth as possible. I know who I want to take over as head, but we will of course go through the usual consultative process. I want to get this going quickly, however, so that I can have time to phase in the transition properly.

In my day you just took over and had to learn from scratch and pretty much on your own. I spent quite a lot of time trying to figure out how things worked and where you went for what. As much as anything it was the intangible things which were hard to learn. Things like having a *feel* for when is the right time to ask for something, or to introduce a change. *Reading* which way things are going, *anticipating* things happening and being prepared for them. *Knowing* when to plough on and when to concede gracefully. You can't teach those kinds of things, you have to learn them by experience. Even then, experience is no guarantee as some of my colleagues with many years of experience still have to learn them.

I want my successor to be a success and I will do everything I can to show her (if the person I think *should* take over actually does) how I manage things. I believe there is even a course now for new HODs and I will suggest that she thinks about taking it. I have been on a couple of courses and found some of the literature which was given out and some of the activities quite useful. We have also had people from the educational development unit 'facilitate' our departmental retreats. They showed us more material to do with the running of a department and confronting various issues. With the movement towards accountability I believe some HODs nowadays are running surveys to see how they are regarded within the department. That is something she will have to work out for herself. However, I can take her around to meet people I have found particularly helpful and whose opinions I have often sought and valued. There are a couple of senior HODs who are particularly valuable.

As I relinquish the headship and membership of university and faculty committees, I can keep my eyes open for opportunities to serve on national or international research committees. This is what I used to do, and it is the area in which I want to re-establish myself. When I start re-establishing contact with my colleagues, especially as I start travelling and attending international and national conferences, then I can look for possible openings, let people know that I am back on the scene and the type of involvement I am looking for. So this coming year will be one of easing off in terms of my local (or institutional) responsibilities, and re-establishing and taking up opportunities for involvement in national and international professional societies, research councils or similar level committees.

- I will start the process of consultation for a new HOD and then plan for a systematic transfer. I will actively plan to make the transition as smooth as possible.
- As I ease out of local responsibilities I will do all that I can to re-establish or make new links with people in the national and international bodies where I see myself playing a role up to and after retirement.

Your turn

We have considered some aspects of 'other responsibilities' which may or may not be of relevance to you. We have also seen the people depicted in the case studies trying to work their way through their concerns in these areas. Now it is your turn to try to make sense of your 'other responsibilities' and to consider the part you see these playing as your academic career develops. As with past exercises, it is a good idea to make notes as you consider the questions which follow.

- *What are my other responsibilities?*

Make a list of your 'other responsibilities'. To do this you may wish to consult the categorization given earlier in this chapter. Is this of any use to you? For example, can you categorize your other responsibilities into: administration, external academic work and external earnings? If so, use these general headings and then draw up a list of the tasks you undertake *within* each general heading. Think of other areas of your work which you have not considered so far. For example, did you consider clinical work when you looked at your teaching, and did you consider your consulting activities under research? Are you satisfied that you have now covered the major aspects of your role as an academic?

- *How do I see 'other responsibilities' in terms of my overall career development in the future?*

Look at the list you have produced. Have the activities you have outlined become more or less important to you relative to teaching and research? If you have already allocated time percentages to teaching, research and other responsibilities, reconsider these for a moment. After working through this chapter, do you wish to change the figures? What do the figures tell you about the place you would like to see 'other responsibilities' occupying in your career, and about the way you actually allocate your time?

- *How are my 'other responsibilities' changing and developing? How should they be?*

Look again at your list of other responsibilities. Work through each responsibility or task and mark it according to whether it is growing (G), stable (S) or declining (D). Now work through the list once more and allocate priorities. If the task is one which you think it important that you keep up or develop, mark it with a tick. If it is a task which you would like to relinquish, mark it with a cross. What pattern of involvement do you have presently, and what general or overall changes would you like to see to this pattern in the future?

- *What new areas of responsibility would I like to move into?*

As you have worked through this chapter have you come across any areas in which you are *not* presently involved but where you think you could or should participate in the future? Which areas are these and why do you consider a move into them could be of value to you?

- *What evidence do I have by which I might evaluate my other responsibilities?*

Take in turn each present or possible future task or responsibility you have identified. Make a note of any evidence you might have with which to document and evaluate your work in each area. Think of the groups or individuals that are affected by your work in each area and make a list of them. How could you go about finding out how they regard your performance in the area? Is it a matter of simply asking individuals for feedback 'face-to-face' or would a survey be more appropriate? Could you use a blend of methods? If there are a number of areas which you wish to document and evaluate, make a plan to do so over the next three years (do not try to do everything at once).

- *What specific plans can I make regarding my other responsibilities?*

Work through each of your other responsibilities again and make a note of any thoughts you have with regard to specific developments or plans for particular activities. For example, Michael (Michelle) Richards is planning for the development of consultancies as his research project progresses; Janet (John) Smith is planning to become publications officer for her

WHAT ABOUT MY OTHER RESPONSIBILITIES? 121

international society; Paul (Pauline) Whiting is planning to start a newsletter, to become chair of the admissions committee and to make changes to its operation; Charles (Carol) Ross is making specific plans to ease the transition of a new head of department. Outline specific plans regarding each area of your own responsibility.

- *How can I make time for and better integrate my other responsibilities?*

Can you determine a pattern for your other responsibilities throughout the year? Are there certain times of the year when certain tasks come up and if so, can you anticipate these now and allocate time for them in your year planner? Can you allocate time not only to perform the task itself, but also to evaluate and reflect on how it has gone over the year? Is there any way for you to better integrate the activities which fall under 'other responsibilities' with your teaching or research? Can you, for example, conduct research and publish on any of these activities, or use anything which has come through them to inform and contribute to your teaching? In what ways could you build such links?

- *How can I develop my knowledge or skills?*

Again, in considering the tasks and responsibilities which you have indicated as playing a part in your future career and which you wish to develop, is there anything you can do to prepare yourself or provide yourself with skills which will help you to accomplish these tasks? Janet (John) Smith, for example, is going to learn some facilitation skills to help her become less domineering and authoritarian in meetings (and tutorials). Paul (Pauline) Whiting will attend a course and find out more about becoming an appraiser. How could you develop in the areas which you have identified as being important to you?

- *What about the appraisal interview?*

In the appraisal interview, how far do you wish to disclose your long- and short-term objectives and plans with regard to the responsibilities you have outlined above? What will be your overall stance towards this area in the interview, what do you wish to discuss, what objectives and plans will you put forward? Will you outline those areas which are growing, stable, declining, and the priorities you have assigned to areas which you wish to keep up or to shed? Can you justify the direction you are taking? What do you anticipate will be your appraiser's attitude towards your participation in the activities you have outlined? Is it likely that he or she will be positive and encouraging, or negative? Do you wish to bring up any matters concerning resources, funding, space, equipment, training or development with the appraiser? What will you ask for; how will you justify your requests?

Note

1 The work of Ingrid Moses and Earnest Roe is especially helpful with respect to headship. Moses and Roe (1990) provide a good starting point in charting the

dimensions of headship, the functions, skills and responsibilities of the position and areas of potential tension and conflict. A shorter and more practically oriented guide by the same authors is Moses and Roe (1989). Paul Dressel's (1981) book on administrative leadership is useful in providing an American perspective.

Chapter Nine

How will the appraisal interview go?

Introduction

In this chapter we will look at what you can do to prepare for an appraisal interview, and offer some advice to help you in successfully negotiating the interview. I have said repeatedly that it is up to you to decide how far you intend to bring the insights you develop as you work through this book into your appraisal interview. I hope that this chapter will allow you to appreciate various aspects of the appraisal interview, irrespective of your decision.

We will start by considering some of the things you can do to prepare for the appraisal interview, making sure that the aims of the interview are clearly appreciated by both yourself and the appraiser and that both the topics to be covered and the paperwork have been satisfactorily negotiated. The setting for the interview is considered next and some guidelines are given on what to do in order to avoid a poor environment for the discussion. Some pointers are then advanced as to how the discussion should proceed, the role you should expect to play and what you can expect of your appraiser. Some aspects of poor appraiser behaviour are also noted and you are encouraged to watch out for these and intervene if necessary.

Finally, there is a consideration of the outcomes of the appraisal interview, recapping and clarification of what has been agreed and the clear identification of implications for resources and workload. It is suggested that you take the lead in writing up the outcomes and that you clearly understand the process whereby your requests relating to resources or workload are considered and decided.

Preparing for the appraisal interview

For the most part, and despite severe misgivings before the interview, it is probably fair to say that most people find the appraisal experience beneficial, at least the first time around. If this has *not* been your experience, then you should consider some of the issues raised below, and try to effect changes in the future. The main reasons for a person leaving an appraisal interview feeling dissatisfied are:

- misunderstanding of the purpose of the appraisal interview by either the appraiser or appraisee;
- inadequate preparation on the part of the appraiser or appraisee;
- poor setting for the appraisal interview;
- failure of the appraiser and appraisee to develop a reasonable relationship due to such things as personal antipathy or lack of trust, respect, openness and honesty.

Of these, the last is of fundamental importance. If you can build a good relationship with your appraiser, then you will be able to confront any of the other problems which emerge during the process. Having a forward looking and developmentally-oriented appraisal scheme also helps enormously. So too does the ability of the appraisee to have some say in determining who will be the appraiser. However, even the most assessment-oriented, hierarchical and bureaucratic of schemes (which were common in the early days of appraisal in higher education) can be subverted to produce positive outcomes when appraisers and appraisees are able to openly and honestly discuss the process of appraisal. Let us take each of the areas which can cause problems in turn.

Paperwork

The most important thing that can be said about paperwork is that it is supposed to help you *develop* as a teacher, researcher, administrator, etc. That may be hard to believe. Some of the forms which have been produced clearly indicate a misunderstanding of what the process *should* be about. The worst of these are little more than checklists, in which the individual has to rate him or herself on pre-determined criteria and scales. The predominant orientation is towards what has happened in the past or is now happening; the forms are directed towards 'performance assessment'.

The uniform information yielded by such forms may be easy to handle bureaucratically, but appraisal should not have bureaucratic control as its focus. If it does, the appraisal process becomes an annual, routinized chore, undertaken by individuals for no other reason than that it is required. They do not see it as helping them and in fact it wastes their time. It is for someone else's benefit in keeping a check on them. The paperwork should, therefore, allow you to express what is important for you, to make your own self-evaluations and plans on your own terms and in your own language. It can legitimately be argued that the best appraisal form an institution can adopt is a blank sheet of paper.

If you are dissatisfied with the appraisal form your institution is using, say so, see if others agree with you, and try to negotiate a better system. You can start by attempting to do this with your appraiser. An example of how an institutional scheme may be out of step with the requirements of staff is given by Gibbs *et al.* (1989). They reproduce a typical annual review form (taken from a former polytechnic) as shown in Figure 9.1.

Figure 9.1 *Example of a typical annual review form*

Annual Review Form
1   In-house job development
1.1   Course development
1.2   Personal skills development
1.3   New administrative responsibilities
2   Publications
3   Research
4   Papers presented at conferences
5   Short courses and conferences attended
6   Consultancy and professional practice
7   Local community activities
8   Membership of committees
9   Work for degrees and other qualifications
10   Other activities (eg, development of overseas links)
11   Polytechnic/departmental resources received in support of staff development activities

Source: Gibbs *et al*. (1989).

It might be worthwhile comparing the categories used in your own institution with this scheme. Gibbs *et al.* (1989) make the point that this scheme 'does not contain a single item concerned with teaching, even though teaching is the main activity of most lecturers' (p. 153). They then offer an alternative scheme to correct the deficiency; this is shown in Figure 9.2.

The point then, is that you should view the paperwork associated with an appraisal scheme as being a starting point, rather than a *fait accompli*. By all means use the categories of your institutional appraisal scheme as a guide or structure for your thoughts, but do not let it inhibit the *real* process of appraisal, whereby you come to know yourself better and make plans for your future development.

You can try to negotiate with your appraiser the form of the paperwork and the categories which will be used. This suggests that you should have a meeting with your appraiser *before* the appraisal interview takes place. There are other things which you may discuss with your appraiser at this meeting, concerning the aims of the interview and the setting. A preliminary meeting also offers a good opportunity to demonstrate that you are taking the process seriously and that you are taking time to prepare thoroughly. It is to be hoped that your appraiser will recognize these messages and respond accordingly.

Figure 9.2 *An alternative annual review form*

Appraisal of teaching for the year ....
1   **Steps taken to improve teaching methods/skills**, eg, attendance at seminars, short courses or conferences concerned with teaching, observation of your own or others' teaching, support from educational development unit, development projects undertaken, etc.
2   **Teaching, learning and assessment methods introduced**, including changes made in response to previous appraisal.
3   **Course and teaching evaluation evidence collected**, eg, summaries and data from questionnaire surveys undertaken, with comparative data from other courses or previous years if possible.
4   **Scholarship concerned with teaching**, eg, regular reading of journals concerned with the teaching of your subject, presentation of conference paper on teaching, research project based on your teaching, publication of article on teaching, etc.
5   **Planned changes in your teaching**, including steps to achieve these changes, eg, application for financial support, visits to other institutions or conferences.

Source: Gibbs *et al*. (1989).

Aims of the appraisal interview

You should read carefully the documentation which normally accompanies appraisal forms and in which the aims of the appraisal interview are set out. These will often suggest that the process is designed to encourage and assist in your personal and professional development. Most appraisers will have undergone some kind of training activity in which the developmental focus will have been clearly spelled out. The trouble is that the actual paperwork may not reflect the intent, and some appraisers simply may not have accepted the developmental focus. We have already considered how you might go about negotiating the paperwork. This can set the scene for discussing with your appraiser what you see as the main aims and focus of the interview.

Also included in the documentation which you receive should be a clear statement concerning the confidentiality of material, what happens to the paperwork after the interview, the purposes it can legitimately be used for and who is eligible to see it. Again, these matters can be confirmed at a preparatory meeting before the interview.

The setting

In the preliminary discussion you can raise the question of where the interview will take place. Many appraisers, especially after training exercises, realize that holding the interview in their own room can immediately set the wrong tone. Physical settings often mirror status positions and hierarchy. The worst situation is for the appraiser to sit in a high, comfortable chair, behind his or her large desk, with the appraisee summoned to sit on a low chair, in this 'alien' and intimidating environment.

We tend to be most comfortable in familiar surroundings, and so if the appraiser does not suggest it first, you might offer your own room for the discussion, if this is feasible. You can explain that all your files are there if you need to look up something. Failing that, a comfortable tutorial room or some other 'neutral territory' might suit. Whatever the venue, you should try to minimize the hierarchical or 'power' arrangement of the room as far as possible. A good solution is for you both to sit on similar chairs on the same side of a table which you can both use to lay out your notes and documents. Alternatively, comfortable chairs and a coffee table might suffice. In the preparatory meeting you can also arrange the date for the interview and say that you will clear a given amount of time (perhaps an hour and a half) for the meeting, that you will divert (or unplug) your phone, and ask not to be interrupted during the time set aside.

All of these measures can help the interview proceed smoothly, by emphasizing that it is a process whereby a *colleague* helps you to consider your own position and development in the future. As this colleague plays such a pivotal part in the process, it is worth considering some aspects of the appraiser's role in a little more detail.

The appraiser

My own experience of training appraisers suggests that the majority are very concerned to play a facilitative role and genuinely have the interests of their appraisees at heart. Many would have preferred not to have had the responsibility thrust upon them and many are concerned that they lack the required skills to succeed. There is, of course, no simple 'blueprint' for an appraiser to follow. Those who perform the role well will bring with them an ability to blend the many skills they have learned in relating to people over their lifetimes.

Watch your appraiser, note what he or she does to try and put you at ease and make the interview go smoothly. If you are not doing so already, you may yourself be called upon to play the part of appraiser one day. Observing and reflecting on the process you experience offers a good opportunity for you to undertake some important, if unintentional, professional development in this area.

In most appraisal training exercises, the idea of a beginning, middle and end to the appraisal interview will have been advanced. The beginning is concerned with the appraiser trying to put you at ease and making sure that you both agree on what is supposed to happen and what ground is to be covered. The middle is the substantive discussion and the end is concerned with the clarification and recording of what has been decided, and who will do what next. Achieving rapport at the beginning is fundamental to what follows. Anything you can do to help in this is obviously to your own advantage.

It may be that you already know your appraiser well and have a good relationship with him or her. If you do not, try to get to know the appraiser *before* the formal process begins. Both you and your appraiser should be trying to strike up a personal and professional relationship which extends further than a required yearly interview. It might be worthwhile for you to undertake a little 'homework' before trying to get to know your appraiser better, and certainly before the preparatory meeting or the appraisal interview itself. What is the appraiser like as a person? Can any of your colleagues fill in some details here? For example, they may tell you that your appraiser, whom you always assumed to be diffident and aloof, is in fact quite sociable and has a good sense of humour. You may now begin to see your appraiser in a different light.

Is there anything else you can find out about your appraiser, perhaps regarding background, where the appraiser comes from, or the professional associations to which he or she belongs? Are there any points of contact here that you can note, or perhaps others such as mutual friends or acquaintances, hobbies, conferences you have attended, courses you teach, etc? Your appraiser should be trying to put you at ease when the appraisal interview begins; the more you can assist in this process of establishing rapport, the better.[1]

Process of the discussion

Monitoring the discussion

Let us suppose that you have successfully completed the preparatory meeting and have managed to set up the appraisal interview along the lines suggested. Let us also suppose that the preliminaries of the actual interview are over and that you have now come to the substantive, middle section.

You should be taking the lead in evaluating how you think things have gone over the past year, and how the insights you have gained from this illuminate the objectives and plans you have for the coming year. The main focus should be forward looking and self-directed, with the role of the appraiser being to facilitate, assist and clarify, rather than to assess and judge.

It is of course up to you to decide whether you want to share with the appraiser the long-term view of your career you may have gained from completing the questions in the earlier chapters of this book. If you believe that there is a sufficient degree of rapport and trust existing between you, then the appraisal interview can offer a good opportunity to ask for a second opinion on where you see yourself going, the difficulties you may face and the actions which you think are necessary in order to take you there. Sharing your long-term view can help to put in context and make sense of your more immediate objectives.

Skilled appraisers will spend most of the interview listening carefully to what you say. They will allow you to expand and explain your plans and will encourage you by asking open-ended questions such as: 'Where do you see yourself going with your research?', rather than closed questions such as, 'How many papers will you publish next year?' They will listen intently to what you have to say, and not immediately interpret what you say to talk about their own experiences or prejudices. They will try to understand you.

You too should try to do the same when your appraiser speaks. Try not to hear only the first few words and immediately think that you know exactly what the appraiser is saying. This is called 'self-listening', and occurs when you are listening more to your own thoughts than to what the other person is actually saying. Attentive listening is a difficult, active and demanding skill. As you listen you are doing a number of complex things all at the same time. For example, you may be *skimming* (listening only casually); *surveying* (to obtain an outline); *sorting* or *categorizing* (into conceptual frameworks); *searching* (for particular content); *memorizing* (words or phrases for your response); *applying* (to different circumstances); *analysing* or *evaluating* what is being said. Do not jump to premature conclusions. Try to suspend judgement and response until you are sure that you have completely understood what the appraiser is saying. What you immediately interpret as a criticism may be no more than a general observation. If you are in doubt, ask for clarification.

A poor appraiser will spend too much time talking. An interview can get off to a bad start if the appraiser asks a closed question, such as the one above concerning how many papers you intend to publish, and you respond in an equally closed manner with: 'Two papers'. The appraiser might then say, 'In which journals?', to which you again reply factually. A pattern has begun to develop with the appraiser taking the active role of questioner and you being forced into the passive role of respondent. Be aware of this danger and if something like this happens, intervene to change the nature of the conversation. You might, for example, say something like: 'In order to answer that perhaps I should say something about . . . '.

Other things to watch for in the attitude taken by the appraiser are the 'halo' effect and 'just like me'. In the former, the appraiser might generalize from either good or bad performance in one area to others, which are quite separate. Thus, just because you have a good publication record, it does not follow that your teaching is equally strong. If you feel confident in the appraiser, be prepared to be critical of yourself in the different aspects of your work. In 'just like me' the appraiser may continue to interpret everything that you say in terms of the way that his or her own career has progressed. Again, be prepared to note what the appraiser says, but to draw distinctions between this and your own position. *Your* development is the focus of the discussion, irrespective of whether or not it follows that of your appraiser.

Finally, appraisers may have taken the message of training sessions to heart, and be so intent not to impose their own agenda on the discussion that they offer virtually *no* advice or comment during the interview. In this case, and where you would really value their opinion, do not be afraid to ask for it.

Making notes and monitoring time

As the discussion proceeds you will need to make a note of what has been decided with regard to each area discussed. For example, when you have finished talking about teaching and getting the appraiser's view of your plans, you will need to note exactly what it is that you intend to do over the coming year or further if your discussion has considered the longer term. Make sure that your plans in this area are clear before moving on to the next.

Natural breaks such as these also present a good opportunity to gauge how the discussion is going with regard to time. If it looks likely that you will run out of time then you have a number of options. You may be able to agree with the appraiser that you should continue past the time set aside for a mutually agreed amount of extra time, if that is possible. Alternatively, you may want to suggest that the agenda for this meeting is abbreviated, perhaps taken in a different order to that intended, and that you reconvene to consider the rest of the agenda at a further meeting in the next day or so.

Avoid simply running out of time and thus giving inadequate coverage to particular aspects of your work. Remember, this may be one of the few times during the year when you have the opportunity to discuss the development of your career and your own professional development. Make sure you receive the time to which you are entitled.

Concluding the interview

The main points to have emerged from the discussion should have been noted at the end of each section. The conclusion of the interview should now be a fairly straightforward matter of recapping and confirming these. Different appraisal schemes have differing formulas for the completion of paperwork. As the whole point of the exercise is to assist you and your development, it is highly desirable that *you* take responsibility for writing up the outcomes of the discussion. Even if your appraisal scheme insists on the appraiser completing the paperwork, you might suggest that you produce a draft from which the appraiser can then work. In the preparatory meeting you should have confirmed where the documentation goes, who has access to it and for what purposes. It is just as well to corroborate this once more before the interview ends.

Arising from the discussion may be implications for resources and workload. For example, it may have been agreed that you should ask for funding to attend a conference, upgrade your computer system, buy software, develop a new course, seek assistance from a colleague in teaching an existing course, increase the number of tutorials for a course or seek funding for laboratory demonstrators. It is important that you are clear on how such requests will be taken up.

Many appraisers are also heads of departments, and they are placed in a difficult position when requests concerning resources and workloads emerge in an appraisal interview. This is one of the main problems of hierarchical appraisal, where appraisers have to assume two different, and sometimes contradictory, roles. During the appraisal interview they should be facilitating and encouraging the appraisee and their developmental plans for the future. For example, an appraiser may genuinely have agreed that you *need* to attend a conference in order to promote your research profile, or that you really do need more resources to cover the extra tutorials which your course demands.

You should be aware, however, that in the role of head of department, appraisers also have requests concerning workloads and resources from other members of staff, following these appraisal interviews. It is unrealistic to expect HODs in appraisal interviews to commit themselves with respect to resources and workloads, even though they may genuinely agree that your proposals are sound and desirable. Your requests should enter a pool containing all the other requests, and be decided according to departmental (or institutional) priority. Some HODs simply decide such matters themselves, others put in place delegated or democratic procedures. The most you may be able to hope for at this stage is the appraiser's (HOD's) agreement that your requests *are* reasonable and desirable, together with a clear understanding of how they will be weighed in comparison with those of your colleagues, and how and when the final decision will be made.

Summary checklist

Here is a checklist which you might want to refer to as an *aide-mémoire* in preparing yourself for an appraisal interview.

Preparing for the interview

- Get to know your appraiser and help in the development of rapport.
- Set up a preliminary meeting.
- Negotiate the agenda, topics to be covered and paperwork.
- Show that you are taking the matter seriously by thorough preparation and scheduling sufficient time for both preparation and discussion.
- Be familiar with the appraisal scheme, including confidentiality, who has access to the paperwork and for what purposes.
- Agree on a suitable setting and avoid use of the setting and furniture layout to confirm status.
- Ensure sufficient time has been cleared for the interview.
- Divert or unplug phones, forestall interruptions.

During the interview

- Learn from the experience and the appraiser's handling of it.
- Expect to take the lead in the discussion and to do most of the talking.
- Maintain a forward looking and developmental focus.
- Practise attentive and active listening.
- Watch out for stereotyping, 'halo' and 'just like me' attitudes from the appraiser.
- Take one section at a time, consolidate, agree and make a note.
- Be aware of time and take action if time looks like running out.

Concluding

- Recap and confirm outcomes at the end.
- Write up and complete the paperwork yourself.
- Be clear on resource and workload requests.
- Check what happens next with regard to resource and workload requests.

And finally

The tenor of this book has been that the appraisal interview *can* offer an opportunity for lecturers to systematically review, set objectives and make plans with regard to their careers, teaching, research and other responsibilities. In fact, in preparing for an appraisal interview, lecturers may find new purpose, new direction and renewed enthusiasm as they rethink, re-evaluate and take control of their professional lives. On the other hand the appraisal interview may also be seen as a site of contest. At worst, manipulative managerialist interests may try to institute surveillance and increase their powers of authority in order to control and direct. This is obviously anathema to a concept of professionalism in which autonomous individuals are given wide discretion to practise and develop their skills within a framework of professional principles and conscience.

With this in mind I would like to register two hopes. First, I hope that by working through this book you will be in a stronger position to take the field when the time for appraisal interviews comes round again. Perhaps you have been able to interpret your own present career position in a slightly wider context than previously and have looked to the future with somewhat more conviction than before. Perhaps you have considered evaluating your teaching, research and other responsibilities a little more rigorously than was formerly the case. Perhaps you have a better idea of exactly where you intend to be going with each of these in the future. If so, the professional self-knowledge you have developed may place you in a stronger position to seize the opportunity provided by the appraisal interview and to bring forward your own agenda; to be able to clearly articulate what your plans are and what support you need from your department and institution.

My second hope is that working through the book may have provided a valuable first step towards your own professional development. I commented that there are now many professional development resources available to lecturers in higher education and that these include not only books and journals but also professional development societies and, increasingly, staff or educational development professionals working from units within institutions. If you can utilize the relationships you have with colleagues and build on these in cooperative projects then so much the better. My second hope is, therefore, that you are able to follow through on the insights you have gained from this book and either individually, or collectively, make contact with professional development materials and people. If it turns out that both of these hopes are realized, then this must augur well for the future of our profession.

Note

For more advice on preparing for an appraisal interview see Gibbs *et al.* (1989) pp. 155–7 and 161–2.

Appendix I

Student evaluation of teaching (institutional)
Thurs, June 4, 1993   Dr E Garwood   31 Students
ARAB 103 (Term 3)

This form gives you an opportunity to indicate your reaction to this course and the way it has been taught. Student opinion is a valuable guide in course planning and in evaluating teaching.

In the questions below, the word 'course' refers to the paper or part of a paper identified in the heading of this questionnaire.

When considering the questions, please try not to let your overall reaction to the course prevent you from noting areas of strength or weakness. Circle the number which best indicates your reaction.

1. Overall, how valuable do you think this course has been for you?

extremely valuable	very valuable	moderately valuable	slightly valuable	not at all valuable
1	2	3	4	5

2. How well organized have you found Dr Garwood's contribution to this course?

very well organized	well organized	moderately well organized	disorganized	very disorganized
1	2	3	4	5

3. How would you rate Dr Garwood's ability to communicate ideas and information?

excellent	very good	good	fair	poor
1	2	3	4	5

4. How much has Dr Garwood stimulated your interest in the field?

very much	quite a lot	moderately	a little	not at all
1	2	3	4	5

5. How would you describe Dr Garwood's attitude toward students in this course?

very helpful	helpful	moderately helpful	rather unhelpful	very unhelpful
1	2	3	4	5

6. Overall, how effective have you found Dr Garwood in teaching this course?

very effective	effective	moderately effective	rather ineffective	very ineffective
1	2	3	4	5

Appendix II

Calculation of results from a student evaluation of teaching

The *mean* (or average) is a measurement which can be used to give an idea of the central tendency of student responses on a rating scale. However, means tend to be affected (ie, pulled up or down) if there is a small number of responses at either extreme of the scale. When this happens, the mean does not give a very good indication of central tendency.

A simple *median* (the middle or 50 per cent point of the responses) is not affected by extreme response. However, it yields only a crude measurement in the form of a whole number. The only value which the median could take would be the whole number category values of 1, 2, 3, 4 or 5, and most people would probably score 2 or 3.

The calculation described here is for an *interpolated median*. This allows for a finer level of discrimination than 1 or 2, for example, while maintaining the median property of not being overly influenced by a small number of extreme responses. The method is explained below by showing examples of 'long hand' calculations. A computer programme can obviously facilitate calculation.

- Count the frequency of response in each category of the rating scale and convert it to percentages. Take the following, for example:

1. Overall, how valuable do you think this course has been for you?

extremely valuable	very valuable	moderately valuable	slightly valuable	not at all valuable
1	2	3	4	5
40 responses	60 responses			
40%	60%			

- Starting from 1, find the category which contains the median (the half way or 50 per cent mark). In this example the median is obviously in category 2, 'very valuable'. Assume that the responses in category 2 are evenly spread out from 1.5 to 2.5.
- Again, starting from 1, there are 40 per cent of cases up to 1.5. To find the 50 per cent mark, the median, we need to add to these another 10 per cent of the cases

136

which are spread between 1.5 and 2.5. So, 1.5 + 10 per cent of the 60 per cent of cases between 1.5 and 2.5 is: 1.5 + 10/60 = 1.67. This gives a more discriminating measurement than the simple 2 of the common median. Here are some more examples:

1	2	3	4	5
10% of	30% of	50% of	10% of	0% of
responses	responses	responses	responses	responses

The median (50 per cent mark) lies in category 3. Counting from category 1, 40 per cent of responses lie between here and 2.5 (10 per cent + 30 per cent). This leaves the last 10 per cent to be taken from category 3, where the 50 per cent is assumed to be evenly distributed between 2.5 and 3.5. So, 2.5 + 10/50 = 2.70.

1	2	3	4	5
0% of	0% of	0% of	20% of	80% of
responses	responses	responses	responses	responses

The median (50 per cent mark) lies in category 5. Counting from category 1, 20 per cent of responses lie between here and 4.5. This leaves the last 30 per cent to be taken from category 5, where the 80 per cent is assumed to be evenly distributed between 4.5 and 5.5. So, 4.5 + 30/80 = 4.88.

1	2	3	4	5
70% of	30% of	0% of	0% of	0% of
responses	responses	responses	responses	responses

The median (50 per cent mark) lies in category 1. The response in category 1 is assumed to be evenly distributed between 0.5 and 1.5. The 50 per cent mark in category 1 is therefore: 0.5 + 50/70 = 1.21.

Appendix III

Example of results from a student evaluation of teaching

1. Overall, how valuable do you think this course has been for you?

Response	Number	Per cent	Median	Std Dev.
1 extremely valuable	3	11		
2 very valuable	1	4		
3 moderately valuable	22	79		
4 slightly valuable	1	4		
5 not at all valuable	0	0		
No response	1	4		
			2.93	0.68

2. How well organized have you found Dr Garwood's contribution to this course?

Response	Number	Per cent	Median	Std Dev.
1 very well organized	1	4		
2 well organized	18	64		
3 moderately well organized	6	21		
4 disorganized	1	4		
5 very disorganized	1	4		
No response	1	4		
			2.19	0.78

3. How would you rate Dr Garwood's ability to communicate ideas and information?

Response	Number	Per cent	Median	Std Dev.
1 excellent	5	18		
2 very good	9	32		
3 good	10	36		
4 fair	1	4		
5 poor	2	7		
No response	1	4		
			2.44	1.07

4. How much has Dr Garwood stimulated your interest in the field?

Response	Number	Per cent	Median	Std Dev.
1 very much	8	29		
2 quite a lot	16	57		
3 moderately	1	4		
4 a little	2	7		
5 not at all	0	0		
No response	1	4		
			1.84	0.79

5. How would you describe Dr Garwood's attitude toward students in this course?

Response	Number	Per cent	Median	Std Dev.
1 very helpful	7	25		
2 helpful	7	25		
3 moderately helpful	9	32		
4 rather unhelpful	2	7		
5 very unhelpful	0	0		
No response	1	4		
			2.29	0.95

6. Overall, how effective have you found Dr Garwood in teaching this course?

Response	Number	Per cent	Median	Std Dev.
1 very effective	12	43		
2 effective	9	32		
3 moderately effective	2	7		
4 rather ineffective	5	18		
5 very ineffective	0	0		
No response	0	0		
			1.72	1.10

Appendix IV

Comments on a colleague's teaching contribution

I would very much appreciate it if you would give me honest and constructive comments on my teaching, under some or all of the headings below. I will use the comments to help review my own performance [and may choose to use them for institutional decision making within the university]. I will seek your permission in advance before making any other use of your comments. Please feel free to ask me for additional information (eg, course outlines, examples of teaching materials) if you think this would be useful.

Signed (person seeking comment):

1. Academic quality of course content of courses taught (eg, up-to-date, appropriate level and workload, producing students with good skills and knowledge).

2. Appropriateness and standard of procedures to assess students.

3. Administration related to teaching (eg, course coordination, record-keeping, advising students).

4. Availability and helpfulness to individual students.

5. Efforts in course development and improvement of teaching.

6. Supervision of postgraduate and other research students.

7. Commitment to teaching.

8. Perceived overall effectiveness as a teacher.

Name of person providing comments:

Position held:

Signature:

Date:

If you do not wish your comments to be used for institutional decision making (eg, application for promotion) please strike out that purpose (the portion in square brackets) in the introduction to this questionnaire.

Appendix V

Student evaluation of teaching (developmental): questions for student feedback

STUDENT OUTCOMES AND EFFORT

OVERALL

1. How valuable do you consider this course has been for you? Extremely valuable 1 2 3 4 5 Not at all valuable

KNOWLEDGE AND INTELLECTUAL SKILL

2. How much do you feel you have learned or accomplished in the course? A great deal 1 2 3 4 5 Very little

3. I have become more competent in this area due to this course: To a great extent 1 2 3 4 5 Not at all

4. How much factual material did you learn in this course? A great deal 1 2 3 4 5 Very little

5. Did this course improve your understanding of concepts and principles in this field? Yes, greatly 1 2 3 4 5 No, not at all

6. Can you now identify main points and central issues in this field? Yes, clearly 1 2 3 4 5 No, not very well

7. Did you gain skill in applying principles from this course to new situations? Yes, greatly 1 2 3 4 5 No, not at all

8. How valuable was this course in terms of developing new skills and techniques? Extremely valuable 1 2 3 4 5 Not at all valuable

9. Did you improve your ability to solve real problems in this field? Yes, greatly 1 2 3 4 5 No, not at all

10. I developed the ability to recognize good arguments in this field: To a great extent 1 2 3 4 5 Not at all

11. Did you improve your ability to evaluate research in this field? Yes, greatly 1 2 3 4 5 No, not at all

12. Did you improve your ability to carry out original research in this field? Yes, greatly 1 2 3 4 5 No, not at all

13. How much has this course improved your judgement? Greatly 1 2 3 4 5 Not at all

14. Has this course encouraged you to develop original ideas? Yes, greatly 1 2 3 4 5 No, not at all
15. This course enhanced my creative abilities: Greatly 1 2 3 4 5 Not at all
16. Did you improve your ability to communicate clearly about this subject? Yes, greatly 1 2 3 4 5 No, not at all
17. Has your ability to express ideas in writing been strengthened through this course? Yes, greatly 1 2 3 4 5 No, not at all

INTEREST AND CURIOSITY

18. Did this course increase your interest in the subject matter? Yes, greatly 1 2 3 4 5 No, not at all
19. I enjoyed learning about this subject matter: Very much 1 2 3 4 5 Not at all
20. Has this course stimulated your interest in taking additional related courses? Yes, greatly 1 2 3 4 5 No, definitely not
21. Were you stimulated to discuss course topics with friends outside of class? Yes, often 1 2 3 4 5 No, never
22. How much extra reading about the course material were you stimulated to do? A large amount 1 2 3 4 5 None
23. Did your interest in this course increase or decrease as the course progressed? Greatly increased 1 2 3 4 5 Greatly decreased
24. How much did this course challenge you to think? A great deal 1 2 3 4 5 Very little

SOCIAL AND PERSONAL SKILLS AND ATTITUDES

25. I developed some leadership skills because of this course: To a great extent 1 2 3 4 5 Not at all
26. Did you learn to value new viewpoints because of this course? Yes, definitely 1 2 3 4 5 No, not at all
27. Has this course made you more aware and concerned about societal problems? Yes, greatly 1 2 3 4 5 No, not at all
28. Has this course helped you to understand yourself better? Yes, greatly 1 2 3 4 5 No, not at all
29. Has this course made you more aware of your interests and talents? Yes, much more 1 2 3 4 5 No, not at all
30. Has this course helped you develop a greater sense of professional responsibility? Yes, greatly 1 2 3 4 5 No, not at all
31. Has this course helped you develop more confidence in yourself? Yes, greatly 1 2 3 4 5 No, not at all

STUDENT PARTICIPATION AND EFFORT

32. How much effort did you put into this course? A great deal 1 2 3 4 5 Very little
33. How appropriate was your background or preparation for this course? Very appropriate 1 2 3 4 5 Very inappropriate

34. I prepared before coming to class: Always 1 2 3 4 5 Never
35. How well did you keep up with the   Very well 1 2 3 4 5 Not at all well
    work in this course?
36. How often had you completed   Always 1 2 3 4 5 Never
    assigned reading before discussion in
    class?
37. I sought help when I didn't   Always 1 2 3 4 5 Never
    understand the material:
38. Did you actively participate in class   Yes, often 1 2 3 4 5 No, never
    activities?
39. Did you actively participate in class   Yes, often 1 2 3 4 5 No, never
    discussions?
40. How much suggested or other non-   A great deal 1 2 3 4 5 None
    required reading did you do for this
    course?

INSTRUCTOR SKILLS AND ATTITUDES

OVERALL

41. Rate the contribution of the lecturer   Excellent 1 2 3 4 5 Poor
    to this course:
42. How effective was the lecturer in   Very effective 1 2 3 4 5 Very ineffective
    teaching this course?

ORGANIZATION AND PRESENTATION SKILLS

43. How would you characterize the   Excellent 1 2 3 4 5 Very poor
    lecturer's ability to explain?
44. As a class leader, the lecturer was: Very effective 1 2 3 4 5 Very ineffective
45. Did the lecturer seem well organized   Yes, always 1 2 3 4 5 No, never
    and prepared for classes?
46. The lecturer's knowledge of course   More than adequate 1 2 3 4 5 Inadequate
    topics appeared to be:
47. The lecturer's lectures seemed well   Always 1 2 3 4 5 Never
    organized:
48. The lecturer gave an overview at the   Always 1 2 3 4 5 Never
    start of class presentations:
49. The lecturer summarized material   Always 1 2 3 4 5 Never
    presented in class sessions:
50. The lecturer changed approaches   Always 1 2 3 4 5 Never
    when the occasion demanded it:
51. The lecturer presented material at a   Almost always 1 2 3 4 5 Almost never
    level appropriate to the class:
52. The lecturer seemed to sense when   Almost always 1 2 3 4 5 Almost never
    students did not understand:
53. The lecturer recognized students'   Almost always 1 2 3 4 5 Almost never
    difficulties in understanding new
    material:
54. The lecturer varied the tempo of the   Very well 1 2 3 4 5 Very poorly
    class to suit the content and student
    needs:
55. The lecturer clearly indicated what   Always 1 2 3 4 5 Never
    was important to learn in each class
    session:
56. The lecturer's presentations allowed Almost always 1 2 3 4 5 Almost never
    me to take good notes:
57. The lecturer's presentation of   Very clear 1 2 3 4 5 Very unclear
    abstract ideas, concepts and theories
    was:

58. The lecturer was able to explain difficult material to my satisfaction: Almost always 1 2 3 4 5 Almost never
59. The lecturer was able to answer questions clearly and concisely: Almost always 1 2 3 4 5 Almost never
60. The lecturer clearly explained relationships among course topics: Frequently 1 2 3 4 5 Never
61. Where possible, the lecturer broke down complex topics for easier explanation: Always 1 2 3 4 5 Never
62. The lecturer explained new ideas by relating them to familiar concepts: Often 1 2 3 4 5 Seldom
63. Did the lecturer make good use of examples and illustrations?   Yes, often 1 2 3 4 5 No, very seldom
64. The lecturer's examples were usually: Very appropriate 1 2 3 4 5 Inappropriate

BASIC COMMUNICATION SKILLS

65. The lecturer's use of the blackboard was: Very effective 1 2 3 4 5 Very poor
66. The lecturer's use of the overhead projector was: Very effective 1 2 3 4 5 Very poor
67. I could clearly hear what the lecturer was saying: Almost always 1 2 3 4 5 Almost never
68. Was the lecturer's speech easy to understand?   Very easy 1 2 3 4 5 Very difficult
69. The lecturer generally spoke: Too fast 1 2 3 4 5 Too slowly
70. The lecturer looked at the class while speaking: Most of the time 1 2 3 4 5 Rarely
71. The lecturer exhibited annoying mannerisms: Frequently 1 2 3 4 5 Never

MOTIVATION AND STIMULATION

72. The lecturer stimulated my interest in the subject: Very much 1 2 3 4 5 Not at all
73. Did the lecturer help motivate you to do your best work?   Yes, very well 1 2 3 4 5 No, not at all
74. The lecturer stimulated my intellectual curiosity: Frequently 1 2 3 4 5 Almost never
75. How interesting were the lecturer's presentations?   Very interesting 1 2 3 4 5 Very boring
76. In this course, I felt challenged and motivated to learn: Almost always 1 2 3 4 5 Almost never
77. The lecturer held the attention of the class: Very well 1 2 3 4 5 Very poorly
78. How enthusiastic did the lecturer seem to be about teaching this course?   Very enthusiastic 1 2 3 4 5 Very unenthusiastic
79. Did the lecturer relate course content to recent developments/issues, where possible?   Yes, frequently 1 2 3 4 5 No, hardly ever
80. The lecturer used humour effectively: Frequently 1 2 3 4 5 Never
81. Did the lecturer encourage students to think for themselves?   Yes, consistently 1 2 3 4 5 No, not at all
82. The lecturer encouraged development of new viewpoints and appreciations: Very much 1 2 3 4 5 Very little
83. The lecturer encouraged students to develop their own ideas and approaches to problems: Frequently 1 2 3 4 5 Never

DISCUSSION AND STUDENT INVOLVEMENT

84. Was class discussion a valuable part of this course?

Yes, very valuable   1 2 3 4 5   No, of little value

85. Did the lecturer raise challenging questions in class?

Yes, very often   1 2 3 4 5   No, seldom

86. Class discussion topics were:

Very well chosen   1 2 3 4 5   Poorly chosen

87. Questions presented to the class to generate discussion were generally:

Too specific   1 2 3 4 5   Too vague

88. The lecturer initiated fruitful and relevant discussions:

Frequently   1 2 3 4 5   Never

89. Class discussion had clear direction and purpose:

Almost always   1 2 3 4 5   Almost never

90. Was a good balance of student participation and lecturer contribution achieved?

Yes, very good   1 2 3 4 5   No, very poor

91. Did the lecturer try to involve all students in class activities?

Yes, consistently   1 2 3 4 5   No

92. How often was discussion monopolized by only one or a few students?

Almost always   1 2 3 4 5   Almost never

93. How often did the lecturer encourage interaction among students?

Frequently   1 2 3 4 5   Never

94. How often did the lecturer encourage class members to work as a team?

Frequently   1 2 3 4 5   Never

95. Was the lecturer receptive to differing viewpoints or opinions?

Yes, always   1 2 3 4 5   No, never

96. The lecturer encouraged students to present their own opinions or experiences:

Frequently   1 2 3 4 5   Never

ATTITUDES TOWARD, AND RAPPORT WITH, STUDENTS

97. How would you describe the lecturer's attitude toward students in the course?

Very helpful   1 2 3 4 5   Indifferent

98. Did the lecturer treat students fairly and with respect?

Yes, always   1 2 3 4 5   No, never

99. Did the lecturer seem genuinely concerned about each student's progress?

Yes, very much so   1 2 3 4 5   No, not at all

100. How conscientious was the lecturer about his or her teaching responsibilities?

Very conscientious   1 2 3 4 5   Very negligent

101. Did the lecturer promote an atmosphere conducive to work and learning?

Yes, very much so   1 2 3 4 5   No, not at all

102. The relationship between lecturer and class generally seemed:

Comfortable   1 2 3 4 5   Tense or hostile

103. Did the lecturer's personality interfere with his or her teaching?

Yes, a great deal   1 2 3 4 5   No, not at all

104. The lecturer was sensitive to student needs and concerns:

Almost always   1 2 3 4 5   Almost never

105. How patient was the lecturer in working with you?

Very patient   1 2 3 4 5   Very impatient

106. How helpful was the lecturer to students with problems?

Very helpful   1 2 3 4 5   Not at all helpful

107. How accessible was the lecturer to students outside class hours?

Very accessible   1 2 3 4 5   Very inaccessible

108. Did the lecturer seem willing to spend extra time with students?	Very willing	1 2 3 4 5 Very unwilling
109. Evaluations of my work were made in a constructive manner:	Almost always	1 2 3 4 5 Almost never
110. The lecturer praised student efforts, where appropriate:	Frequently	1 2 3 4 5 Never
111. Students felt free to interrupt presentations if points needed clarification:	Always	1 2 3 4 5 Never
112. The lecturer listened attentively to what class members had to say:	Always	1 2 3 4 5 Never
113. Students could debate with each other or the lecturer in a non-threatening atmosphere:	Always	1 2 3 4 5 Never

COURSE ORGANIZATION, COMPONENTS, REQUIREMENTS, AND MATERIALS

COURSE PLANNING AND ORGANIZATION

114. The course seemed:	Very well organized	1 2 3 4 5 Very disorganized
115. What the lecturer expected of students was:	Very clear	1 2 3 4 5 Very unclear
116. Was there agreement between announced course objectives and what was taught?	Strong agreement	1 2 3 4 5 Little agreement
117. Did the lecturer follow a course outline?	Yes, very closely	1 2 3 4 5 No, not at all
118. Teaching methods used in this course seemed:	Very well chosen	1 2 3 4 5 Poorly chosen
119. The lecturer coordinated the different activities of this course:	Very well	1 2 3 4 5 Very poorly
120. The balance among activities (lectures, practical work, reading, assignments, etc.) was:	Very satisfactory	1 2 3 4 5 Very unsatisfactory
121. Topics and activities were presented in a logical and coherent sequence:	Almost always	1 2 3 4 5 Almost never
122. Do you feel the lecturer needs to plan the use of class time better?	Yes, much better	1 2 3 4 5 Definitely not
123. Did you feel class time was spent on unimportant and irrelevant material?	Yes, often	1 2 3 4 5 No, never
124. Should more/less class time be used to review and synthesize course material?	Much more time	1 2 3 4 5 Much less time
125. The amount of class time allotted to question and discussion was:	Much too great	1 2 3 4 5 Much too small
126. Classroom facilities were:	Very good	1 2 3 4 5 Very poor
127. The number of students in the class was:	Too large	1 2 3 4 5 Too small
128. How effectively was team teaching used in this course?	Very effectively	1 2 3 4 5 Very ineffectively
129. The different lecturers coordinated their teaching:	Very well	1 2 3 4 5 Very poorly
130. How did lectures relate to material in textbooks and other readings?	Too much overlap	1 2 3 4 5 Too unrelated
131. Should the lecturer give the class more or less direction and guidance?	Much more guidance	1 2 3 4 5 Much less guidance
132. Would you appreciate more advice on how to study for this course?	Yes, much more	1 2 3 4 5 No

COURSE CONTENT

133. What is your opinion about the objectives for this course?	Very well chosen 1 2 3 4 5 Poorly chosen
134. How do you view the orientation of course content?	Too theoretical 1 2 3 4 5 Too applied
135. How do you view the level of course content?	Too advanced 1 2 3 4 5 Too elementary
136. How difficult was the course material for you?	Much too hard 1 2 3 4 5 Much too easy
137. How do you view the scope of the course?	Much too broad 1 2 3 4 5 Much too narrow
138. In my view, the course attempted to cover:	Much too much 1 2 3 4 5 Much too little
139. How suitable for you was the pace of the course?	Much too fast 1 2 3 4 5 Much too slow
140. Did this course repeat material which you had been taught in other courses?	Yes, considerably 1 2 3 4 5 No, not at all

OVERALL COURSE WORKLOAD

141. How much work did this course require?	Much too much 1 2 3 4 5 Much too little
142. The amount of work outside class required for this course was:	Very excessive 1 2 3 4 5 Very small

ASSIGNMENTS, PROBLEM SETS AND PROJECTS

143. The time and effort devoted to completing written assignments was:	Very well spent 1 2 3 4 5 Wasted
144. Regular small problem sets or assignments were:	Very valuable 1 2 3 4 5 Worthless
145. Regular small problem sets or assignments were:	Very demanding 1 2 3 4 5 Straightforward
146. How worthwhile did you find the written assignments (essays, reports, etc.)?	Very worthwhile 1 2 3 4 5 Worthless
147. Did the written assignments (essays, problem sets, etc.) seem well chosen?	Yes, very well 1 2 3 4 5 No, poorly
148. The time and effort required by written assignments was generally:	Too great 1 2 3 4 5 Too little
149. How well did your lecturer relate assignments to other aspects of the course?	Very well 1 2 3 4 5 Very poorly
150. How did you find the written assignments?	Very stimulating 1 2 3 4 5 Boring
151. Did the lecturer permit enough freedom in choosing topics for assignments?	Ample freedom 1 2 3 4 5 Too little freedom
152. Were you given sufficient creative freedom in writing assignments?	Yes, plenty 1 2 3 4 5 No, too little
153. Were instructions for assignments clear and specific?	Yes, always 1 2 3 4 5 No, never
154. Would you have appreciated more guidance on how to write good assignments?	Yes, much more 1 2 3 4 5 No
155. Adequate time was allowed for completing assignments:	Always 1 2 3 4 5 Never
156. Were written assignments returned promptly?	Yes, always 1 2 3 4 5 No, never

157. The major project was: Very valuable   1 2 3 4 5   Of little value
158. The degree of emphasis placed on   Much too great   1 2 3 4 5   Much too small
     the major project was:
159. The assignments/projects have   A great deal   1 2 3 4 5   Very little
     improved my understanding of
     concepts and principles:
160. How demanding was the lecturer   Too demanding   1 2 3 4 5   Too generous
     about assignment formats, due
     dates, etc.?

TESTS AND EXAMINATIONS

161. How adequate was the lecturer's   More than adequate   1 2 3 4 5   Clearly inadequate
     guidance in preparing students for
     tests/exams?
162. How many tests/exams were given?   Too many   1 2 3 4 5   Too few
163. The tests/exams were generally: Too difficult   1 2 3 4 5   Too easy
164. How would you rate the lecturer's   Excellent   1 2 3 4 5   Very poor
     test/exam questions?
165. Were test/exam questions worded   Yes, very clearly   1 2 3 4 5   No, very unclearly
     clearly?
166. How well did test/exam questions   Very well   1 2 3 4 5   Very poorly
     reflect the content and emphasis of
     the course?
167. Were the lecturer's test questions   Very much so   1 2 3 4 5   Not at all
     thought-provoking?
168. To what extent did tests/exams seem   A great deal   1 2 3 4 5   Not at all
     to test trivia?
169. Were tests/exams marked and   Yes, always   1 2 3 4 5   No, never
     returned promptly?

GRADING AND FEEDBACK

170. The grading procedures for the   Very fair   1 2 3 4 5   Very unfair
     course seem:
171. Did the lecturer evaluate your work   Yes, definitely   1 2 3 4 5   Definitely not
     in a constructive and conscientious
     manner?
172. How well was the grading system for   Very well   1 2 3 4 5   Very poorly
     the course explained?
173. Should the final exam count more or   Much more   1 2 3 4 5   Much less
     less than it does, in your opinion?
174. The lecturer's standards when   Too generous   1 2 3 4 5   Too demanding
     grading student work seemed:
175. How would you characterize the   Very objective   1 2 3 4 5   Very subjective
     lecturer's grading?
176. Were written assignments graded   Yes, very fairly   1 2 3 4 5   No, very unfairly
     fairly?
177. Did quality seem to count more than   Yes, definitely   1 2 3 4 5   Definitely not
     quantity when work was graded?
178. Were the lecturer's comments and   Very helpful   1 2 3 4 5   Not at all helpful
     criticisms about your work helpful?
179. Were exams and assignments   Yes, always   1 2 3 4 5   No, never
     returned with errors explained and/
     or helpful comments?
180. Did you understand why you   Yes, always   1 2 3 4 5   No, never
     received the grades you did on
     assignments?
181. How well were test/exam answers   Very well   1 2 3 4 5   Inadequately
     explained to the class, after the test?

182. The amount of feedback on my progress during the course was: More than adequate   1 2 3 4 5   Inadequate
183. In commenting on student work, did the lecturer suggest specific ways to improve?   Yes, frequently   1 2 3 4 5   No, never

READING MATERIALS

184. Overall, rate the course reading materials (texts, assigned readings, handouts, etc.):   Excellent   1 2 3 4 5   Very poor
185. Rate the main textbook used in this course: Excellent   1 2 3 4 5   Very poor
186. I found the main textbook: Very useful   1 2 3 4 5   Useless
187. I found the main textbook: Very interesting   1 2 3 4 5   Very boring
188. Rate the secondary textbook used in this course: Excellent   1 2 3 4 5   Very poor
189. I found the secondary textbook: Very useful   1 2 3 4 5   Useless
190. I found the secondary textbook: Very interesting   1 2 3 4 5   Very boring
191. The cost of required textbooks and other supplies was: Much too high   1 2 3 4 5   Very reasonable
192. The amount of time and effort required for reading course material was: Much too great   1 2 3 4 5   Very reasonable
193. Were assigned or suggested readings well selected?   Yes, all very good   1 2 3 4 5   No, all very poor
194. Describe the assigned reading: Stimulating   1 2 3 4 5   Boring
195. The assigned reading was generally: Very difficult   1 2 3 4 5   Very easy
196. Were reading assignments well related to class presentations?   Yes, always   1 2 3 4 5   No, never
197. Were appropriate reading suggestions given for different parts of the course?   Yes, consistently   1 2 3 4 5   No, never
198. Regular class preparation work (reading, etc.) suggested by the lecturer was: Very beneficial   1 2 3 4 5   Just busy work
199. Would you have appreciated more guidance on how to use the library?   Yes, much more   1 2 3 4 5   No
200. How useful was the list of references which was handed out?   Very useful   1 2 3 4 5   Useless
201. Would you have appreciated more guidance on how to use the list of references?   Yes, much more   1 2 3 4 5   No
202. How much did suggested (but non-required) reading help your learning and understanding?   Greatly   1 2 3 4 5   Not at all
203. How difficult was it to get access to the reference materials for this course?   Very easy   1 2 3 4 5   Very difficult
204. How valuable were the lecturer's handouts as aids to learning?   Extremely valuable   1 2 3 4 5   Useless

AUDIO-VISUAL MATERIALS

205. The audio-visual materials used in this course were: Very helpful   1 2 3 4 5   Of little help
206. Did audio-visual materials appear to be carefully prepared or chosen?   Yes, always   1 2 3 4 5   No, never
207. Audio-visual materials were integrated with the rest of the course: Very well   1 2 3 4 5   Very poorly

208. How relevant were films and other audiovisual materials to course objectives?

Very relevant   1 2 3 4 5   Very irrelevant

209. Were films a valuable part of this course?

Yes, very much so   1 2 3 4 5   No, not at all

210. Were the films used in this course interesting and stimulating?

Yes, consistently   1 2 3 4 5   No, never

211. Were videotapes a valuable part of this course?

Yes, very much so   1 2 3 4 5   No, not at all

212. Were the videotapes used in this course interesting and stimulating?

Yes, consistently   1 2 3 4 5   No, never

213. Were slides a valuable part of this course?

Yes, very much so   1 2 3 4 5   No, not at all

214. Were the slide presentations interesting and stimulating?

Yes, consistently   1 2 3 4 5   No, never

215. Were tape-slide programmes a valuable part of this course?

Yes, very much so   1 2 3 4 5   No, not at all

216. Were tape-slide programmes interesting and stimulating?

Yes, consistently   1 2 3 4 5   No, never

217. Were language lab experiences a valuable part of this course?

Yes, very much so   1 2 3 4 5   No, not at all

218. Were language lab experiences interesting and stimulating?

Yes, consistently   1 2 3 4 5   No, never

219. Was enough time allocated to interpreting or discussing films or videotapes?

Yes, plenty   1 2 3 4 5   No, too little

LABORATORY CLASSES AND FIELDWORK

220. Did labs seem a valuable part of this course?

Yes, very valuable   1 2 3 4 5   No, worthless

221. How interesting and stimulating were the lab activities?

Very interesting   1 2 3 4 5   Very boring

222. Did lab assignments generally require you to think?

Yes, very much so   1 2 3 4 5   No, not really

223. Lab activities generally seemed:

Too difficult   1 2 3 4 5   Too easy

224. The time and effort required to complete lab work seemed:

Very reasonable   1 2 3 4 5   Very unreasonable

225. In my view, the lab sessions were:

Too long   1 2 3 4 5   Too short

226. Did you have adequate time to complete the lab work?

Yes, always   1 2 3 4 5   No, never

227. How well were labs coordinated with lectures?

Very well   1 2 3 4 5   Very poorly

228. Did the lecturer relate lab work to information from readings and lectures?

Yes, regularly   1 2 3 4 5   No, never

229. Did the lab supervisor seem well prepared for laboratory sessions?

Yes, always   1 2 3 4 5   No, never

230. Were the demonstrators well prepared to answer questions about labs?

Yes, always   1 2 3 4 5   No, never

231. How consistently was adequate individual help available in the laboratory?

Almost always   1 2 3 4 5   Almost never

232. Were you given adequate instructions for proceeding with lab work?

Yes, always   1 2 3 4 5   No, never

233. Rate the laboratory manual or textbook assigned for this course:

Excellent   1 2 3 4 5   Very poor

234. How reliable did you find the lab equipment?   Very reliable 1 2 3 4 5 Very unreliable

235. Did writing lab reports help you learn about relevant theory and experimental methods?   Yes, greatly 1 2 3 4 5 No, very little

236. How much background and detail was demanded in the lab reports?   A reasonable amount 1 2 3 4 5 Far too much

237. Was laboratory work graded promptly, fairly and constructively?   Yes, consistently 1 2 3 4 5 No, never

238. Rate the field trip(s) as a learning experience: Very valuable 1 2 3 4 5 Worthless

239. Rate the conduct of the field trip(s):   Well organized 1 2 3 4 5 Poorly organized

TUTORIALS AND SEMINARS

240. Did tutorials/seminars contribute to your understanding of this subject?   Yes, greatly 1 2 3 4 5 No, not at all

241. On the whole, my tutorials/seminars in this course proved: Very stimulating 1 2 3 4 5 Very boring

242. Was there ample opportunity to ask questions in tutorials/seminars?   Yes, definitely 1 2 3 4 5 Definitely not

243. Was there ample opportunity for you to participate in tutorials/seminars?   Yes, definitely 1 2 3 4 5 Definitely not

244. The amount of outside preparation required for tutorials/seminars seemed: Excessive 1 2 3 4 5 Very modest

245. Did the tutorials/seminars increase or decrease your interest in this subject?   Increased greatly 1 2 3 4 5 Decreased greatly

246. I feel that the contribution of the tutor to tutorials/seminars was: Excellent 1 2 3 4 5 Very poor

247. I found the experience of preparing and leading a seminar myself was: Very worthwhile 1 2 3 4 5 Worthless

248. I found the seminars prepared and led by other students were generally: Very worthwhile 1 2 3 4 5 Worthless

249. How well were the tutorials/seminars coordinated with the lectures?   Very well 1 2 3 4 5 Very poorly

250. Was written work for tutorials/seminars graded promptly, fairly and constructively?   Yes, definitely 1 2 3 4 5 Definitely not

Appendix VI

Head of department feedback evaluation form
Professor Henrietta O'Driscoll, Department of Administration

Introduction
As outlined at our last meeting I am circulating a questionnaire to all departmental academic staff to provide me with feedback on my performance. I will be grateful if you would return your completed questionnaire by January 28 to the secretary of the educational development unit. The forms will be analysed by the unit to ensure that anonymity is preserved.
*Here are some roles and responsibilities which I perform as head of department. Please indicate how satisfied you feel about my performance in each role, by circling the number which best represents your feeling. **If you feel that a particular question does not apply to you, please leave that line blank.***

1 = Very satisfied
2 = Satisfied
3 = Undecided
4 = Dissatisfied
5 = Very dissatisfied

1. Conducting departmental meetings   Very satisfied   1 2 3 4 5   Very dissatisfied
2. Developing long-range plans for the department   Very satisfied   1 2 3 4 5   Very dissatisfied
3. Implementing long-range plans for the department   Very satisfied   1 2 3 4 5   Very dissatisfied
4. Serving as advocate for the department   Very satisfied   1 2 3 4 5   Very dissatisfied
5. Reporting departmental accomplishments to the dean and others in the university   Very satisfied   1 2 3 4 5   Very dissatisfied
6. Improving and maintaining the department's image and reputation   Very satisfied   1 2 3 4 5   Very dissatisfied
7. Providing strong leadership   Very satisfied   1 2 3 4 5   Very dissatisfied
8. Being decisive   Very satisfied   1 2 3 4 5   Very dissatisfied
9. Delegating some administrative functions to others   Very satisfied   1 2 3 4 5   Very dissatisfied
10. Supporting delegated decisions   Very satisfied   1 2 3 4 5   Very dissatisfied

11. Initiating and coordinating activities with outside groups — Very satisfied 1 2 3 4 5 Very dissatisfied

12. Consulting staff and encouraging them to communicate ideas on departmental matters — Very satisfied 1 2 3 4 5 Very dissatisfied

13. Involving staff in the decision-making process of the department — Very satisfied 1 2 3 4 5 Very dissatisfied

14. Considering staff members' points of view — Very satisfied 1 2 3 4 5 Very dissatisfied

15. Selecting new staff members — Very satisfied 1 2 3 4 5 Very dissatisfied

16. Seeking additional university resources — Very satisfied 1 2 3 4 5 Very dissatisfied

17. Assigning responsibilities to staff — Very satisfied 1 2 3 4 5 Very dissatisfied

18. Evaluating staff performance for promotion — Very satisfied 1 2 3 4 5 Very dissatisfied

19. Commending achievement — Very satisfied 1 2 3 4 5 Very dissatisfied

20. Dealing effectively with unsatisfactory staff performance — Very satisfied 1 2 3 4 5 Very dissatisfied

21. Keeping staff informed of departmental and university plans — Very satisfied 1 2 3 4 5 Very dissatisfied

22. Providing staff individually with the opportunity to talk over matters of concern to them — Very satisfied 1 2 3 4 5 Very dissatisfied

23. Treating members of staff equally — Very satisfied 1 2 3 4 5 Very dissatisfied

24. Supporting staff and maintaining morale — Very satisfied 1 2 3 4 5 Very dissatisfied

25. Trusting in the ability of staff — Very satisfied 1 2 3 4 5 Very dissatisfied

26. Reducing, resolving and preventing conflict among staff members — Very satisfied 1 2 3 4 5 Very dissatisfied

27. Advising, counselling and liaising with students — Very satisfied 1 2 3 4 5 Very dissatisfied

28. Encouraging staff to seek research funding — Very satisfied 1 2 3 4 5 Very dissatisfied

29. Stimulating research and publication — Very satisfied 1 2 3 4 5 Very dissatisfied

30. Encouraging participation in professional bodies — Very satisfied 1 2 3 4 5 Very dissatisfied

31. Encouraging good teaching in the department — Very satisfied 1 2 3 4 5 Very dissatisfied

32. Encouraging all staff to perform at a high standard — Very satisfied 1 2 3 4 5 Very dissatisfied

33. Taking account of each staff member's special talents and interests — Very satisfied 1 2 3 4 5 Very dissatisfied

34. Discussing, with you, the ways in which you might improve performance — Very satisfied 1 2 3 4 5 Very dissatisfied

35. Discussing, with you, your career ambitions and how they might best be achieved — Very satisfied 1 2 3 4 5 Very dissatisfied

36. Generally, taking everything into consideration, how satisfied are you with my performance as head of department? — Very satisfied 1 2 3 4 5 Very dissatisfied

Could you please write down your feelings about my performance as head of department under the following headings?

37. What do you consider to be by strengths as head of the department?

38. In what ways could I make changes to improve my performance as head of department?

39. Any additional comments?

Bibliography

Abramowitz, S I, Gomes, B and Abramowitz, C V (1975) 'Publish or politic: referee bias in manuscript review', *Journal of Applied Social Psychology*, 5, 187–200.

Aisenberg, N and Harrington, M (1988) *Women of Academe*, Cambridge, Mass.: University of Massachusetts Press.

Beattie, K (ed.) (1993) *So Where's Your Research Profile? A resource book for academics*, Melbourne: Union of Australian College Academics.

Becher, T (1989) *Academic Tribes and Territories. Intellectual enquiry and the cultures of disciplines*, Buckingham: The Society for Research into Higher Education and Open University Press.

Bligh, D (1990) *Higher Education*, London: Cassell.

Boyer, E L (1990) *Scholarship Reconsidered. Priorities of the professoriate*, Princeton, NJ: The Carnegie Foundation for the Advancement of Teaching.

Canadian Association of University Teachers (1978) *Guide to the Teaching Dossier: its preparation and use*, Montreal: Centre for Teaching and Learning Services, McGill University.

Cashin, W E (1990) 'Student ratings of teaching: a summary of the research', *Management Newsletter*, 4, 1, 2–7.

Ceci, S J and Peters, D B (1984) 'How blind is blind review?', *American Psychologist*, 39, 1491–4.

Chapman, A J (1989) 'Assessing research: citation-count shortcomings', *The Psychologist: Bulletin of the British Psychological Society*, 8, 336–44.

Ciccheti, D V and Conn, H O (1978) 'Reviewer evaluation of manuscripts submitted to medical journals', *Biometrics*, 34, 728.

Cohen, P A (1981) 'Student ratings of instruction and student achievement: a meta-analysis of multisection validity studies', *Review of Educational Research*, 51, 3, 281–309.

Cole, S, Cole, J R and Simon, G A (1981) 'Chance and consensus in peer review', *Science*, 214, 881–6.

Dressel, P L (1981) *Administrative Leadership. Effective and responsive decision making in higher education*, San Francisco, CA: Jossey-Bass.

Eisner, E (1985) *The Art of Educational Evaluation. A personal view*, London: Falmer Press.

Endler, N S, Rushton, J P and Roediger, H L (1978) 'Productivity and scholarly impact (citations) of British, Canadian and US departments of psychology (1975)' *American Psychologist*, 33, 1064–83.

Feldman, K A (1987) 'Research productivity and scholarly accomplishment of college teachers as related to their instructional effectiveness: a review and exploration', *Research in Higher Education*, 26, 3, 227–98.

Fox, M F (1983) 'Publication productivity among scientists', *Social Studies of Science*, 13, 2, 285–305.

Garfield, E (1974) 'Citation indexing for studying science', *Nature*, 227, 669–71.

Gibbs, G (1989) *Creating a Teaching Portfolio*, Bristol: Technical and Educational Services Ltd.

Gibbs, G, Habeshaw, S and Habeshaw, T (1989) *53 Interesting Ways to Appraise your Teaching*, Bristol: Technical and Educational Services Ltd.

Gitlin, A and Smyth, J (1989) *Teacher Evaluation: Educative alternatives*, London: Falmer Press.

Halsey, A H (1992) *Decline of Donnish Dominion. The British academic professions in the twentieth century*, Oxford: Clarendon Press.

Kingman, J (1993) 'The pursuit of truth', *The Times Higher Education Supplement*, 18 June, p.15.

Knefelkamp, L L (1990) 'Seasons of academic life', *Liberal Education*, 76, 3, 4.

Marsh, H W (1987) 'Students' evaluations of university teaching: research findings, methodological issues, and directions for future research', *International Journal of Educational Research*, 11, 255–378.

Moore, M (1978) 'Discrimination or favoritism? Sex bias in book reviews', *American Psychologist*, 33, 936–8.

Morrow, J R, Bray, M S, Fulton, J E and Thomas, J R (1992) 'Interrater reliability of 1987–1991 Research Quarterly for Exercise and Sport reviews', *Research Quarterly for Exercise and Sport*, 63, 2, 200–204.

Moses, I (1989) 'Is performance "management" appropriate in a learning institution?', *Journal of Tertiary Education Administration*, 11, 2, 127–41.

Moses, I and Roe, E (1989) *Heading a Department. A guide for heads and chairs of departments and schools*, Kensington, NSW: Higher Education Research and Development Society of Australasia.

Moses, I and Roe, E (1990) *Heads and Chairs. Managing academic departments*, St Lucia, Queensland: University of Queensland Press.

Naftulin, D H, Ware, J E and Donnelly, F A (1973) 'The Doctor Fox lecture: a paradigm of educational seduction', *Journal of Medical Education*, 48, 630–35.

O'Neil, M and Pennington, G (eds) (1992) *Evaluating Teaching and Courses from an Active Learning Perspective*, Sheffield: CVCP Universities' Staff Development and Training Unit.

Over, R. (1993) 'Correlates of career advancement in Australian universities', *Higher Education*, 26, 313–29.

Pennington, G (1992) 'Seven common misconceptions about evaluations of teaching', in O'Neil, M and Pennington, G (eds) *Evaluating Teaching and Courses from an Active Learning Perspective*, Sheffield: CVCP Universities' Staff Development and Training Unit, University of Sheffield, pp. 63–7.

Peters, D B and Ceci, S J (1982) 'Peer-review practices of psychological journals', *Behavioral and Brain Sciences*, 5, 187–95.

Ramsden, P and Dodds, A (1989) *Improving Teaching and Courses. A guide to evaluation*, Melbourne: Centre for the Study of Higher Education, The University of Melbourne.

Robertson, H (1992) 'Teacher development and gender equity', in Hargreaves, A and Fullan, M (eds) *Understanding Teacher Development*, London: Cassell, pp. 43–61.

Rudd, E and Hatch, S R (1968) *Graduate Study and After*, London: Weidenfeld & Nicolson.

Schwartz, P and Webb, G (1993) *Case Studies on Teaching in Higher Education*, London: Kogan Page.

Scriven, M (1981) 'Summative teacher evaluation', in Millman, J (ed.) *Handbook of Teacher Evaluation*, London: Sage.

Scriven, M (1988) 'The validity of student ratings', *Instructional Evaluation*, 9, 2, 5–18.

Sikes, P J, Measor, L and Woods, P (1985) *Teacher Careers. Crises and continuities*, London: Falmer Press.

Simeone, A (1987) *Academic Women. Working towards equality*, Mass.: Bergin and Garvey.

Smyth, J (1989) 'Collegiality as a counter discourse to the intrusion of corporate management into higher education', *Journal of Tertiary Education Administration*, 11, 2, 143–55.

Startup, R (1979) *The University Teacher and his World. A sociological and educational study*, Hampshire: Saxon House.

Startup, R (1985) 'The changing perspective of academic researchers, 1973–1983', *Studies in Higher Education*, 10, 1, 69–78.

Theodore, A (1986) *The Campus Troublemakers: Academic women in protest*, Houston: Cap and Gown Press.

Welch, L B (ed.) (1990) *Women in Higher Education. Changes and challenges*, New York: Praeger.

Ziman, J (1981) 'What are the options? Social determinants of personal research plans', *Minerva*, 19, 1, 1–42.

Index